Supply Ch

For Small and Me

Bill Waddell
2016

Supply Chain Management for Small and Medium Sized Manufacturers

ISBN13:978-1515068112

ISBN10:1515068110

First Printing: March 2016

Introduction

This book is intended to serve as a guide for the complete design, implementation, control and continuous improvement of the manufacturing supply chain. While it is comprehensive in its scope the professional can and should find a wealth of supplementary information in the vast body of resources available in each specific aspect of supply chain planning and execution. Our primary intent is to provide a single reference for the supply chain as a whole and to assure that both senior management and supply chain professionals understand what the implications of decisions made in any one element of the supply chain might have on the rest of the supply chain, as well as on the company as a whole.

In far too many instances the supply chain is a product of disjointed decisions, often made long ago, and typically made on the basis of detailed accounting numbers that fail to take the entire supply chain into consideration. It is common to see supply chains built to conform to the requirements of a packaged ERP system, rather than in support of company strategy. In effect, organizational leaders have turned the management of the critical backbone of the business over to third party software designers. Our intent with this book is to empower management to take control of the supply chain and to assure it is designed in such a way that it supports company strategy. This book also seeks to assure that management makes critical supply chain decisions with their eyes wide open, understanding all of the financial and performance considerations of what often seem to be innocuous and detailed operational decisions.

The first section, encompassing nine chapters, deals primarily with the strategic, top level supply chain issues. The supply chain, as previously described, is the backbone of the business. It is the sequence of steps that takes raw materials from the source to the end customer, and the role the company plays in this process, defines the company. This is obviously important stuff. We describe the critical decisions regarding vertical integration – what value the company will add and what will be procured from sources further up the chain. Nothing could be more at the heart of management's decision making than this.

We also describe and discuss the financial implications of supply chain architecture decisions. A supply chain built around low cost off-shore sources of supply will tend to have higher fixed expenses to manage such an extensive supply chain, as well as higher investments in inventory and the supporting infra-structure; resulting in a business that is highly sensitive to fluctuations in volume. Conversely, a business which sources from higher cost, local sources will have higher unit costs but a significantly lower investment in inventories, leading to lower costs of material control and handling. That company will be much less sensitive to volume swings. The company that sources off-shore will have lower cost but will be much less responsive to changes in customer demands – in both volume and mix. The domestic sources will probably have higher unit costs but will be more flexible and able to react much quicker. These are critical senior management considerations, and not matters to be determined ad hoc, at lower levels, based on narrow cost accounting analyses.

There are also higher level issues to consider regarding the relationship of supply chain architecture and product management. A wide range of procured items and products will necessarily result in greater inventories. Product life cycles also have a significant impact on inventory planning, management, and risk. Finally, the technology of the products must be taken into account. Suppliers are often an essential source of new technology and can be vital partners in bringing new products to market. Decisions on supplier selection obviously have much broader implications than just standard price-quote based sourcing.

These issues, along with risks and concerns about the investment and operating costs inherent in various execution options are discussed in this first section. The intent is to assure that senior management has made effective decisions concerning the architecture of the supply chain and is able to provide clear direction to the operational people assigned to the myriad of tasks and decisions that are involved in actually bringing the supply chain to life. We cannot stress enough the importance of these strategic considerations. Left untended, the operational people will too often make decisions that are limited by their narrower scope of the business' strategy and will create supply chains that do not support long range strategies.

In short, the supply chain should be designed and continually evaluated in order to assure that it is aligned with, and fully supportive of, company strategy. When this is not done, the supply chain becomes a limiting factor in strategy execution and severely reduces the likelihood of success.

The heart of this book is the second and third sections which encompass inventory planning and control; flow planning and scheduling; factory floor control and execution; alternative approaches; and supplier relationships and logistics.

In this section we will get into the details of the various techniques and technologies used to plan and execute an effective supply chain. In many companies a hybrid of MRP and demand pull (kanban) has grown, with a sprinkling of 'Theory of Constraints' thinking. Each of these well-developed approaches has their own strengths and weaknesses. In some cases they can be applied in a complementary fashion, but quite often they serve conflicting objectives and create confusion and sub-optimization. Choosing the most appropriate technique, or combination of techniques, should follow the strategic decision making process and will have quite a bit to do with the success or failure of the strategy.

Although they can seem to be factory floor minutiae, matters such as lot sizes, machine set-up and change over times, as well as production and supplier lead times are actually huge drivers of supply chain performance. The implications of these factors on inventory and factory execution will be discussed in Section Two.

Supplier relationship techniques and approaches will also be discussed. There is a wide range of ways the company's relationship with its suppliers can be established, ranging from arms-length, one off purchase orders based on individual quotes from a range of potential sources for each P.O. all the way to well developed, almost seamless partnerships. Given that purchased parts and materials are typically the company's single biggest cost category, selecting the most appropriate suppliers and creating an optimal relationship is very important. Execution of the sourcing process is equally critical.

Interwoven throughout all of this is inventory planning and control. Where inventory should be put in place, how much inventory should be kept on-hand, and how it is managed and controlled are critical concerns. Inventory is often the biggest and highest risk investment that a company makes. Too often these inventory decisions are made based on poorly analyzed 'safety stock' decisions. The right amount of inventory is a complicated decision, based on lead times, variations in rates of supply and demand, and lot sizes – both for transportation and production batches.

We will discuss critical control concerns such as purchased material and manufactured item quality. The execution and flow of the supply chain requires well planned and well executed control mechanisms to assure that materials flowing through the supply chain meet specifications and requirements. The design of the quality control system and the supply chain process cannot be treated as independent events, as is too often the case. There are also item, lot and document control considerations in many industries. Manufactured batches must be tracked in food and drug products, individual items or lots of items must be tracked by serial number or lot number for many aerospace, defense and automotive applications. Creating the optimum, most economical flow, while maintaining necessary control of items in the process is no easy task.

Finally, the logistics processes shall be discussed. There are many things to consider in determining how materials will physically flow from suppliers to the factory and from the factory to customers. A number of ground transportation options are available, as well as air and ocean freight alternatives. Each has cost, time and inventory trade-offs and the logistics scheme must be developed holistically, rather than based on one-off freight quotes. Load consolidations – both truckload and container-load – can reduce direct shipping costs, but tend to increase inventory levels and detract from cash flow. Use of techniques such as 'milk run' logistics systems is described as one means of obtaining an optimum combination of inventory and freight costs.

In-sourcing and out-sourcing decisions must be made with the management of the overall process in mind. There are a number of third party logistics options available to every manufacturer, and there are major considerations to take into account when making the decision to use any of them, either in whole or in part.

The last section will include chapters on measuring, controlling and improving the supply chain. Once in place, the operating processes should be tracked and continually monitored. At the most basic level, financial controls must be established to assure this huge driver of company cash flow and profits is being executed well. Unfortunately traditional accounting systems do a poor job of providing the necessary measurements. More creative and holistic financial measurements are available in the Lean Accounting body of knowledge, as well as in the Reshoring Initiative's 'Total Cost of Ownership' model.

The supply chain is a tightly integrated combination of fixed overhead expenses and variable product costs; as well as major balance sheet items – primarily inventories. Traditional cost accounting does not deal with trade-offs between assets, direct costs and allocated costs very well. Further compounding the matter are the various time frames of the cash outflows, ranging from current period costs to long range investments. How to measure the supply chain, taking all of this into consideration, is discussed in this section.

It is said that there is no such thing as non-financial metrics – just financial metrics accounting has not been able to accurately quantify. These include many of the quality performance and cycle time measurements that are perhaps the most critical indicators of supply chain execution. These will be discussed, as well.

The core concept of Lean Manufacturing is continuous improvement and, while this book is by no means a comprehensive guide to Lean, those principles of Lean which directly relate to supply chain optimization are described. Particular attention is paid to techniques such as value stream mapping, hiejunka (one piece flow) and single minute exchange of dies (quick set-ups and changeovers). The application of Six Sigma techniques is described, as well, particularly as it relates to quality control. Tai'ichi Ohno, The chief architect of the Toyota Production System, once described the system by saying, *"All we are doing is looking at the time line, from the moment the customer gives us an order to the point when we collect the cash. And we are reducing that time line by removing the non-value added wastes."* He was describing the continuous reduction of supply chain cycle time and non-value adding expenses. Obviously, the principles of the Toyota system – Lean – are directly applicable to supply chain management and improvement.

Finally, all supply chains carry with them a degree of risk. The risk is directly related to the scope of the supply chain. A complex supply chain which is heavily dependent on foreign sources is extremely risky. It is imperative that management understand the sources of risk and have effective means in place to gage and stay on top of that risk while also having effective counter measures in place in the event that something goes wrong.

For some, this book will be a vital source of information to be read and understood from cover to cover. For others, it will best serve as a reference book to be kept on the shelf and referred to when the need arises in order to understand a particular area of concern.

In each chapter, and when addressing each topic, we have taken pains to be sure to point to the other areas of the supply chain affected by decisions in any one area. The supply chain is a highly complex, thoroughly integrated process. While there is a temptation to break a supply chain down into distinct sub-processes and treat them independently, to do so opens up the probability that isolating and optimizing any one area will create offsetting problems in another area. Supply chain excellence requires a very high level of 'systems thinking' – the ability to see the supply chain as something akin to a very complicated domino chain where every domino is affected by knocking over any other domino.

Preface
The Supply Chain as a System

The problem with supply chain design and execution is that the supply chain is an incredibly complex system that interconnects literally every element of the business. It is like one of those elaborate domino chains we all like to watch – knock over one of the dominos and see everything tip over. This chart below is really a grossly over-simplified representation of the physical flow in what is really a very small organization. Most manufacturers have far more suppliers, operations and customers than this chart indicates – yet even this system is almost indecipherable.

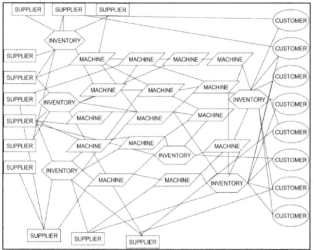

In 1999 Jim Womack, along with others, wrote *"Learning to See – Value Stream Mapping to Add Value and Eliminate MUDA"*. It urged managers to map these complicated processes within their organizations and to learn to manage the business as a system. The book sold well enough, but it has proven difficult for many managers to really grasp and to optimize the complication.

But that is only part of it. In fact, the supply chain is really a series of complex charts like this one, with each customer block serving as an individual supplier block in another complex chart. When Womack et al. followed up a few years later with *"Seeing the Whole: Mapping the Extended Value Stream"* it sailed over just about everyone's head.

It may well have been asking too much to expect people to comprehend and deal with such complexity. But the fact remains that supply chains are complex, integrated systems, and the degree to how well we can manage them depends largely on our ability to think in terms of interconnected systems.

Perhaps the biggest hindrances to effective supply chain management are our accounting systems that support the idea that the business can be broken down into independent chunks – or silos – that can each be managed independently. We create budgets, goals and priorities for each functional group under the assumption that, if each does well with those objectives and measurements, then collectively the whole organization ought to do well. But this doesn't take into consideration the domino effect.

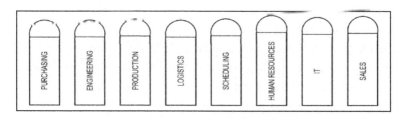

An engineer develops new product (A), containing component B from supplier C to be sold to customer D, and inexplicably the cost of making completely unrelated sub-assembly X with parts from supplier Y and sold to customer Z goes up. Why is that? Changing the mix of products flowing through the factory and the mix of components flowing in from suppliers tips the balance in the plant, changing the capacity constraint from one machine to another which in turn changes the entire flow rate and cost structure of the factory. Or if customer D likes the new product and buys more of it and less of a product that happens to include an unrelated part, but one that also comes from supplier Y and the volumes on the truck from that supplier drop into a worse freight discount category.

We cannot hope to describe and offer a simple way to manage all of this complexity. The best we can do is to point out many of the critical linkages that are in place, and urge managers to view the supply chain with a broad and open mind. Lot sizes from suppliers and the differences in freight rates between truckloads and less than truck loads (LTL) are directly related to the cost and inventory levels throughout the entire supply chain. Purchasing and logistics decisions cannot be made independent of production scheduling and factory optimization decisions. New products cannot be developed with a singular focus on the direct material cost of the product. They inevitably have a ripple effect throughout the entire supply chain that must be considered.

In the end, successful supply chain design, execution, and improvement is a function of management's ability to think in terms of systems – the ability to see as many of the dominos up and down the chain as possible.

Keep in mind that the fundamental systems nature of the supply chain makes this book nearly impossible to write in a linear manner. Finished goods inventory planning cannot be adequately discussed without also discussing production lot sizes and lead times, but production lot sizes and lead times cannot be discussed without also discussing supplier lot sizes and freight cost optimization, and so forth. A book on supply chain management can no more be broken down into neat, independent sections than an organization can be broken down into neat, independent silos. Yet we have to organize the book somehow.

The solution is to ask the reader to read each chapter with an awareness that each chapter relates to the other chapters; they all connect. So if we can do our best to provide the 'hooks' in each chapter that connects its primary topic to the others, and the reader can be on constant lookout for those hooks and links, together we can get our arms around the complicated system your supply chain represents.

SECTION 1
Strategic Considerations

Before the supply chain can be designed or improved senior management level decisions and guidance is an absolute prerequisite. The supply chain is the backbone and central nervous system of the organization – the integrated network of activities that create the value the company provides, and exactly how that value is to be created is a matter only senior people can determine. When left to people in the organization without that senior perspective, the decisions that control how the business operates are very likely to be made in a manner that facilitates a few small corners of the business but miss the basic strategic objectives of the business, drive non-competitive costs and product delivery levels, or otherwise expose the business to levels of risk other than those the senior people are willing to take.

Specifically, the senior people must provide direction regarding:

1. The company's basic strategy
2. The fundamental supply chain model the company wants to adopt
3. Vertical integration
4. Supplier relationships
5. Product and component proliferation strategies
6. Ethical and social considerations
7. Economic guidance
8. The preferred execution model
9. Risk

We have attempted to describe these issues in 'executive summary' form to the degree possible, so it is not necessary for the senior people to read the entire book, but their careful attention to these issues in this first section is vital. Once the issues have been considered and discussed with the people tasked with creating and managing the supply chain, those people can get to work. The more detailed descriptions of each of those issues – and many more – are covered in the rest of the book.

The best approach is for the senior team to read each brief chapter in this first section then meet to discuss and decide on the issues in a manner that reflects a consensus understanding and agreement regarding the organization's goals and supply chain strategy. This way, all of the people throughout the organization who will work within the supply chain can have common direction and a common understanding of what the company is trying to accomplish through its supply chain execution.

Finally, we also urge senior managers to spend some time at the back of the book where supply chain measurements – both financial and non-financial – are discussed.

Chapter 1
The Supply Chain as an Extension of Company Strategy

In many companies – probably most companies – the supply chain 'system' is a complicated collection of detailed computer screens, reports, and practices handed down from one employee to the next. Few, if any, senior managers really understand much about the exact workings of the 'system'. For that matter, few employees actually understand more than their assigned corner of the system – how to schedule their assigned corner of the factory, or what and when to buy for their narrow collection of items. It has a life of its own, developed and evolved over years.

In the early days of MRP (Material Requirements Planning, then known as Manufacturing Resources Planning) – the predecessors of today's ERP (Enterprise Resource Planning) systems people demonstrated mastery of the inner workings of such system with APICS (American Production and Inventory Control Society) certification. While APICS certification has fallen from favor, the underlying idea that knowledge of the inner workings of the supply chain system is something that takes years of study and experience is still very real.

To many senior managers, the supply chain system 'is what it is'; and 'what it is' is not usually something they understand well enough to change in any meaningful way. At best, it is something they manage by setting simple input and output goals – annual targets for purchase price reductions, and inventory reduction goals. More than any other facet of the business, the basic functions and processes of the supply chain are perceived to be a necessary, unchangeable part of doing business. Outsiders suggesting different approaches are often met with the reaction that they simply do not understand the unique nature of the industry and the firm's unique situation; and that the way it is done is the only way it actually can be done.

This collective understanding of the supply chain as an impenetrable and necessary black box that largely exists with a life of its own has a huge limiting impact on company strategy – both in setting strategic plans in place and in executing those plans.

Too often the basic sales strategy – what markets the company will serve, the terms offered to existing and potential customers, the basic cost structure, and even what products the company will offer – are limited by what the monolithic supply chain system has the demonstrated capability of providing. The complicated scheduling machine and its linked purchasing processes support four week lead times, for instance, and it produces in batches or lot sizes of 100 items at a time, generating six inventory turns per year. So a strategy to sell into a new channel, or to sell to a new customer requiring shorter lead times and smaller lot sizes is seen as inevitably requiring greater inventory levels. The basic processes within the supply chain 'system' are limiting factors to strategy, rather than tools to be managed and devised to support and enable strategy.

Where this can be seen most often and most vividly is in far too many manufacturers' inability to use time to their advantage in this era of global competition. Domestic manufacturers are usually unable to compete with an Asian competitor head to head on the basic purchase price of an item, but they should be able to offset that price disadvantage with significant cost savings in other areas resulting from much shorter lead times. The Asian competitor has a built in disadvantage of having to include a month or more of transit time in the total package it offers. This requires the customer to carry quite a bit of inventory, generating the need to incur the cost of owning, storing, managing and protecting all of that stock.

The domestic source should be able to deliver with much shorter lead times, thus saving the customer all of that expense. Too often, however, domestic manufacturers offer lead times not much better than their Asian competitors simply because their basic supply chain concept is not capable of generating shorter lead times. Faced with a choice between eight week lead times from an Asian source, and four weeks from a domestic one, since either alternative creates the need to carry inventory, the nod goes to the Asian source. If the domestic source were to offer lead times measured in days, rather than weeks, however, that would very likely change the total cost equation for the customer. When the only way a domestic producer can see its way clear to do so is to carry all of that inventory itself, the cost ends up built into its own price.

Far too often sales people are tasked with negotiating lead times – attempting to get concessions from customers on price in exchange for

16

shorter lead times, or simply trying to negotiate longer lead times than the customer wants.

In a similar vein, new products are most often limited by the existing supply chain concept. The new product is developed via a stand-alone process, assuming the company will still make what it makes and any new materials or components needed to make the new product are handed off to the sourcing/purchasing function. They are tasked with cutting the best deal they can get from a new source and those new components will be shoved through the supply chain simply as an add-on to all of the existing suppliers and purchased item numbers.

While much of this will be discussed in Chapter 3 when we explore vertical integration – the basic make versus buy strategy of the business - the principle is similar. Supplier selection criteria and supplier relationships can take all sorts of forms. When leadership assumes that only one model is possible – that things must be done the way things have always been done – the products that the firm can offer, and the probability of those new products realizing success in the market are severely limited.

In fact, there is a virtually infinite range of possibilities for supply chain architecture. The company selling a consumer product can sell through the 'big box' retailers that typically demand large, sporadic quantities with very short lead times. Or it can sell directly to customers via the Internet – one item at a time. Or it can sell through a distributor network, usually allowing for longer lead times and quantities somewhere in between the individual units sold via the Internet and the truckloads ordered by the big guys.

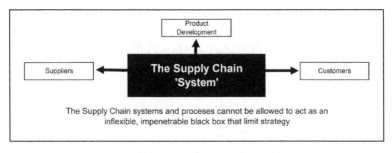

Each channel has profound implications on how the supply chain should be constructed. The structure of the supply chain is flexible, however. There are models and principles to assure success in each of these channels. It is imperative that senior leadership recognize this fact and see the supply chain architecture as an extension of the strategic plan. If the strategy is to expand beyond the current distributor channel and begin to sell directly to the big box retailers then that strategy requires a different set of supply chain principles and a different approach to scheduling. It is apt to require a fundamentally different set of supplier terms and relationships – perhaps even a different set of suppliers. The physical flow of products from the factory is also subject to different concepts of what is optimal – where and how much of the production output should be warehoused is apt to be different – at the factory? In a finished goods warehouse? At regional distribution points? At the customers' facilities?

The good news is that there is no reason why such a strategy cannot succeed, but it is less likely to succeed when the firm attempts to force fit new customers into a 'one size fits all' supply chain strategy.

An excellent example of this in action can be seen in John Deere's foray into consumer products. Long a major provider of agricultural and industrial equipment, Deere decided to leverage their deep knowledge and get into the business of selling lawn mowers to consumers through the likes of the Home Depot and Walmart. They very astutely recognized that, while there were great similarities between consumer lawn mowers and large brush cutting machines in terms of product and manufacturing technologies, there were enormous differences in the supply chains necessary to succeed in the two different channels.

The big, expensive equipment sold to farmers and industrial customers was produced in small quantities with lots of variations in models and options. The consumer business, on the other hand, would consist of relatively few products and variations produced and sold in much larger quantities. Scheduling the factories to make ten units of a hundred different products took a completely different logistical and logical approach than scheduling it to produce five hundred units of two products. It also had significant supplier implications. The wide variation and small quantities in their core business created a need for local suppliers who could make and ship small quantities quickly. The stability and volume of the narrow set of items that go into consumer mowers, coupled with the intense price pressure in consumer products, lent themselves well to foreign sourcing. Even though many of the purchased components were nearly identical for products going into each channel, the best sources were radically different.

Deere's success in penetrating the consumer market certainly was due in large measure to their superior product and strong brand, but it is unlikely to have succeeded without their clear understanding that the supply chain requirements for each channel were markedly different, and their willingness to take an entirely different approach to the supply chain.

There are firms that sell their supply chain management ability as much as they sell products – a number of fastener companies that offer consignment and vendor managed inventory services come to mind, along with industrial supply companies such as Grainger. For the most part, however, the supply chain function limits, rather than enhances, the value proposition. It is imperative that senior leadership recognize this, and take steps to address it. It is not necessary for the senior manager to understand all of the inner working of the systems, but it is necessary for him or her to understand that: (1.) there are basic, underlying principles driving various approaches to supply chain design and execution; (2.) the supply chain strategy of the firm must be driven by the firm's market and product strategy; and (3.) those people tasked with designing and executing the supply chain processes must be provided with clear direction concerning the necessary capabilities of the supply chain needed for the strategy to succeed.

In the subsequent chapters of this first section we will describe the various aspects of the supply chain and their relationship to company strategy, as well as the choice of models and critical inputs that senior management must provide to the people in the organization who are tasked with creating a successful supply chain.

Chapter 2
The Black Box Cost Structure Principle

Perhaps the most fundamental principle behind Toyota's Production System and Lean thinking is the logical, but radically different, rejection of the idea that Cost + Profit (or Margin) = Price. Traditional thinking has held that in order to be profitable the prices charged must include ample margin between the full standard cost and the price to cover administrative expenses and yield a profit. Prices, therefore, are typically calculated on the basis of the 'full' cost plus a margin, and then massaged to fit as closely as possible what is likely to result in a sale.

The rejection of this seemingly logical approach is based on the fundamental economic reality that the market - customers – set prices, not the producers. As a result, the price is not something to be mathematically calculated by the manufacturer so much as it is to be derived from the customers who set prices based on the value they believe the product holds for them. Profit is also not negotiable. It is necessary for the business to survive. This leaves cost as the only input to the equation over which management can exercise any significant control.

Costs are comprised of many elements and most companies focus the majority of their time and effort on the direct, value adding costs of direct labor and purchased, direct materials for the logical reason that these are often the largest areas of cost. At the individual product level they are also typically fairly easy to quantify and measure. However, these costs (1.) typically are difficult to reduce simply because they have been the focus of management attention in the past and most of the low hanging fruit has been picked from them long ago; and (2.) they are the costs of creating value. Customers are generally willing to pay for these costs.

It is in the non-value adding overhead costs that there is typically greater opportunity to reduce costs without detracting from the value of the product. They can often be more difficult to see, however, because they are not directly tied to individual products; rather, they are allocated costs making them seem insignificant at times. They are also mistakenly assumed to be necessary costs of doing business. Too often management simply accepts the basic business processes as the way it has always been, the way it has to be, and the way that everyone does it.

In fact, there are many ways to construct the processes of the business, and the basic supply chain processes are perhaps the single clearest example of this. They are also quite often the single greatest opportunity to significantly change the cost structure of the business. The fact that there is often no clear way to tie the supply chain process expenses to individual products is irrelevant according to Lean thinking. So long as the market driven prices are greater than the direct costs of the products, profits are best driven by reducing the basic cost structure of the business – seeking business processes that consume lower costs. How accounting may need to allocate the lower cost base to individual products for inventory valuation purposes is of no consequence. So long as each product more than covers its direct costs then those products ae contributing to covering the non-value adding costs of running the business and ultimately contributing to profits. As management can lower the cost structure, profits increase regardless of any accounting allocations of overhead.

This is referred to as the 'Black Box" approach because it views the costs of management processes as applicable to the factory as a whole, and not related to any individual products flowing through the factory.

Management's choice of supply chain strategies		Resulting impact on the cost of doing business
Highly structured, comprehensive ERP system with MRP based scheduling	The "Black Box" of the factory	Cost Stucture #1 - $$$
Combination of manual and automated scheduling processes		Cost Stucture #2 - $$
Manual, card driven kanban		Cost Stucture #3 - $

Increasingly, manufacturers are restructuring from traditional functionally based models to value streams. The value stream concept is basically a 'business within a business' approach, in which the business is structured around the different markets it serves and staffed with people with all of the necessary functional expertise needed to optimize value and profits for each market, based on each market's unique perception of value. A manufacturer selling into both the defense and automotive markets, for instance, knows that each of those groups of customers have very different needs. While the product may be quite similar everything from lead time requirements, lot sizes, quality control documentation and billing are apt to be radically different.

The value stream approach enables management to look at the business as comprised of multiple 'Black Boxes' and construct a cost base for each one individually, rather than a 'one size fits all' approach that often drives costs to the lowest common denominator – that is to say, the costliest business processes for each market becomes the cost structure for every market.

The most important point to make is that in making critical decisions regarding the supply chain processes of the business, management is making critical decisions that will determine the basic cost structure of the business. In many cases, the difference between profitable and unprofitable competitors is that the management of the more profitable ones have made better decisions regarding their supply chain architecture.

Chapter 3
Basic Supply Chain Strategy Models

In the most fundamental terms, all firms are either Make to Stock, Make to Order, or a combination of the two. A Make to Order firm is simply a company that procures or produces its products after it receives an order from a customer. A Make to Stock firm is one that procures or produces in advance of customer orders, usually in order to ship very quickly – more quickly than the product can be made available.

The combinations of the two approaches come in a variety of manners. Some companies procure components or raw materials in advance of customer orders – 'purchase to stock' – but do not convert those materials into finished products until a customer order is received. This is typical in firms whose product line consists of a number of different final configurations stemming from common purchased materials. They will buy the material while not knowing for sure which of their end products it will become and wait until the receipt of orders to decide how to configure that material.

Others might offer some products from stock, while other products are not produced until the customer order is received. This approach often makes sense for companies that have a wide range of items with some experiencing high, consistent demand, while others are sold sporadically.

The primary driver of one model versus the other is customer lead time versus the lead time required to procure and produce the product. There are principles to drive the supply chain under each scenario, and it is possible to achieve excellent supply chain performance under each scenario. The starting point is to decide which – make to stock, make to order, or a combination – best supports the strategy the company pursues in the market it serves. Too often, a company tries to achieve make to stock lead times and delivery performance with a supply chain that is designed around make to order products.

In the make to stock environment, there are really two basic approaches to take – demand pull or forecast push. These will be discussed in considerable detail in the second section of this book in which we discuss execution techniques. For the senior manager, however, it is most important to know that the two approaches exist and what their basic characteristics are.

The approach most often used in the past and the one around which MRP and ERP systems were conceived for is forecast push. This approach, as the name implies, involves projecting (forecasting) future demand as far out as the combined lead time to procure and make each product. For example: If the company buys material that requires six weeks for the supplier to deliver after receiving your purchase order, and it takes three weeks for the company to convert the material into finished products, then the company must have a continual forecast of what must be shipped nine weeks into the future in order to know what material should be ordered from suppliers today.

In the example cited, the factory would operate with a firm production plan – often called a Master Schedule – for the next three weeks based on the forecast of demand. Every week the factory would create a new schedule for everything that must be started through production to meet the forecasted customer requirements.

Based on the likely error rate of the forecast, some level of safety stock must be maintained to bridge the gap between what was forecast to be shipped and what customers actually ordered.

The extent to which forecast push is effective, or not, is in direct relation to the degree of forecast error. In cases where future demand is very predictable forecast push can work well. The best cases are those in which there is really not a forecast at all, but rather a plan, such as companies providing components to OEM's that make capital equipment in support of infrastructure projects or long term military contracts. In these cases, the customer has an extensive schedule of requirements well into the future. While there is always the possibility that the schedule might change, it is usually fairly stable and reliable, so the 'forecast' used to push the manufacturer of the components is really the customer's schedule.

However, when future demand is truly unknown then relying on forecasts can result in poor supply chain performance such as excess inventories or missed customer shipment dates. The best examples of this in action are in the retail area where the retailer is compelled to forecast the precise volume and mix consumers will buy in the run up to the holidays several months ahead of time in order to place orders with suppliers from China.

Forecasting consumer demand in detail is a very inexact science and to the extent the forecast is wrong retailers typically have insufficient stocks of popular items, resulting in missed sales opportunities and dissatisfied customers; while at the same time they are left with excess inventories of items in which demand did not meet forecast levels, driving the retailers to offer deep discounts in January and February to get rid of the inventory.

The recent rise of 'rapid retailing' where retailers develop supply chains that are extremely responsive – lead times measured in days or weeks instead of months – in order to reduce their exposure to the negative effects of forecasting errors is a clear example of adapting the supply chain to fit the strategy.

The alternative to forecast push is demand pull. While demand pull can take many forms the basic concept is to put a minimum inventory level in place and then have the purchasing and production functions simply replenish the inventory levels as actual customer demand depletes them. The benefits of demand pull are (1.) simplicity; and (2.) near perfect synchronization of production and procurement with actual customer demand. The demand pull model is the basis for Toyota's 'JIT' (Just In Time) approach that has become widespread in virtually every corner of manufacturing since its inception (at least so far as anyone outside of Toyota knew about it) in the 1980's.

It is a misconception that demand pull only works in high volume, repetitive situations. It can work quite effectively in just about any production or distribution environment. The key to success is in setting the appropriate inventory level from which customer needs are fulfilled and the operations are tasked with replenishing. It is true that the more consistent the customer demand is then the lower the level of required inventory, but such a pull system can be effectively applied under any demand volume and consistency situation.

The naming of the two approaches 'forecast *push*' and 'demand *pull*' simply reflect their fundamental natures. In the push scenario, material is pushed into the supply chain ahead of actual demand; while in the pull scenario customer demand pulls additional material into the supply chain.

It is important to point out that a Make to Order manufacturer is just that – a manufacturer. On the other hand, a Make to Sell company is both a manufacturer and a distributor. Whether the company holds finished goods inventories in a warehouse that it owns in the same building as the factory, or whether the inventory is owned and held by a third party distributor at another location, the issues and implications are the same. In either case, inventory is held between the manufacturer and its customers in order to buffer the gap between the lengthier lead time that the manufacturer has to procure material and make its products, and the shorter lead times customers require. That finished goods inventory can be put in place based on a forecast plus some amount of safety stock to protect against forecast error, or it can be set as a replenishment target in support of demand pull.

The decision to maintain finished goods inventory at the factory, or whether to put it into remote warehouse locations (whether the manufacturer owns and operates the remote warehouses or contracts this out to a third party) is based on transportation lead times. A manufacturer in California, for instance, cannot economically support a customer on the east coast that requires 1-2 day lead times no matter how much finished goods inventory the manufacturer carries. In this case, a warehouse or distribution center within 1-2 days of the east coast customers is necessary, and that warehouse must hold enough inventory to buffer against the manufacturer's procurement and production lead times, as well as the 3-5 day transportation lead time it will take to get finished products from the California factory to the distribution center.

(Another reason for maintaining a geographically separate distribution operation is volume relative to the spread of the customers. For instance, that California manufacturer may have dozens of east coast customers who, while willing to accept the overall lead times, order in frequent, small quantities. It may save transportation costs to ship in bulk – truck loads – to an east coast distribution operation, and then break the shipment down into dozens of relatively short small shipments. Usually, however, this can be accomplished through the freight and logistics arrangements without having to maintain an inventory in a distribution center near the customers.)

These basic policy decisions are the critical first steps in providing direction to those responsible for developing a supply chain that will effectively support the company's overall business strategy:

Should the company be a Make to Order or a Make to Stock business? This depends on the lead time requirements of the customers the company is targeting.

If Make to Stock should the company operate in a forecast push or a demand pull manner? This depends on the reliability of the forecasts and plans the company can expect.

Should the company act as a combined manufacturer and distributor under one roof or should it establish geographically separate distribution operations apart from manufacturing? This depends on the customer locations relative to the factory (or factories) by taking transportation and customer lead times into consideration.

Chapter 4
Vertical Integration Considerations

What to make and what to buy are the most fundamental supply chain decisions that management must make and they are all too often taken for granted. In the not too distant past these decisions were based on theories of 'core competence' and through simple accounting 'make versus buy' cost analyses. There is an increasing awareness that supply chain considerations must also enter into the mix. Simply put, there is a lot more to it than simply making a one-time decision about the firm's 'core competence' and turning the rest over to the accounting department.

Fueled by both globalization and a smaller number of domestic manufacturers is the issue of supply chain risk. The safest way to assure a source of supply is for the firm to produce the necessary materials and components for themselves. Whether this is a good idea or not depends on how easy it would be to find and develop another supplier should anything happen to the primary supplier. If the item is readily available without extensive supplier start up times and expenses, then the risk is relatively low – fasteners and boxes, for instance. On the other hand, if the item in question is only produced by a small number of sources, and switching from one to another would be time consuming and costly, the firm should give serious consideration to developing the capability to produce the item in house.

A primary example of this principle in action is a recent instance of several major automobile companies who were forced to shut down plants and incur millions of dollars in costs as the result of a tsunami in Japan which impacted their sole source for a particular paint. Paint did not fall into what any of them classified as a critical or core competence so we can be assured that their accounting numbers indicated that they were better off buying the paint from the Japanese source than developing the ability to make it themselves. But it is certain that they had no more critical element of their cars than paint when that source was shut down and it would have been worth quite a bit more than their original accounting estimates to have been able to maintain a stable source of supply.

Dual sourcing is also a possible outcome of an ongoing vertical integration assessment, but it too has a down side. The cost of maintaining and supporting two suppliers is very real, even though typical accounting systems do not do a good job of tracking this cost. There is also the very real possibility that by decreasing the volume purchased from the single source that the prices for those items may increase. This reduction in volume often extends through the logistics process, where freight costs may well increase as a result of reduced volumes from a single geographic point.

Another matter of consideration is your supplier's ability to maintain your quality standards. Manufacturing history is littered with examples of companies that suffered in the marketplace and failed all together simply as a result of poor supplier quality. This is most often seen in areas of cosmetic quality – fit and finish specifications that the supplier is simply unable to hold. In many cases the firm is better off in the long term developing by the ability to do the work itself rather than to fight a never ending battle with suppliers over quality.

As the underlying principles of Lean Manufacturing become understood to a much greater degree, many companies are coming to the realization that there is a great deal of benefit to more vertical integration. Not only do they reduce the level of supplier risk and gain greater control over quality but they also decrease total cost in ways not previously understood. Those non-value adding expenses quite often incur at supplier interfaces – the cost of creating purchase orders and paying bills, receiving dock activities, communications costs and so forth. Even more importantly, they are finding that they can bring new products to market much faster and more effectively when they control more of the manufacturing process. They also find that overall cost reduction takes place more effectively when they work intimately with the day to day production of more of their product – they are more likely to identify instances where spending a little more time and money making the component leads to saving an ever greater amount of time and money elsewhere in the production process.

Finally, there is the matter of intellectual property. Many companies have found that, in their pursuit of lower cost suppliers in far off parts of the world, the patents and copyrights which were sufficient enough to protect them locally are difficult to enforce abroad. Anything the company cannot stand to have become open knowledge in China is also a good candidate for vertical integration consideration.

Of course, another option – between insourcing and outsourcing – is a true partnership relationship with critical suppliers. This is an option we will explore further in the next chapter.

The essential takeaway senior leadership should have from this chapter is the necessity to have a carefully considered policy regarding vertical integration on a commodity by commodity basis. It is not enough to simply assert "we are a machining company" or we are a "surface mount company" and outsource everything else; nor is it sufficient to relegate all such decisions to a simple accounting "make" vs "buy" study. There are implications to making components versus buying them that get deep into the strategic realm, and play a large part in how well the supply chain will perform. They include risk assessments of all sorts which will be covered later in the book, as well as the value of control in the effort to continually improve the product.

Chapter 5
Supplier Relationship Strategies

Any honest chef will tell you that their finished product is determined much more by the quality of the ingredients used than by the cleverness of the recipe. Of course, true success requires both. The same is true of manufacturing. Even the most vertically integrated companies rely heavily on their suppliers for their success. In far too many companies, however, purchase price dominates the supplier selection process and that usually comes at the expense of dire consequences to supply chain execution. This is somewhat akin to the most thoroughly trained and capable chef buying all of his ingredients from the cheapest grocer in town. It is not going to generate good results.

Certainly there are some purchased items that are essentially commodities –readily available with short lead times and quality is not much of an issue. Fasteners and boxes again come to mind. In these cases price should certainly be a dominant determiner of the source of supply. In many other cases, however, there is a lot more to it than just price and it is essential that senior leadership play an active role in determining who the company chooses as its source.

The most obvious cases are those in which the supplier provides a critical technology. One has to look no further than that legal battles being waged around the globe between Apple and Samsung – the supplier of some of the core technologies essential to the iPhone – to see the importance of strategic relationships. These relationships will be discussed further in Chapter 6 where we explore product development considerations.

It is also fairly obvious that senior management must set the direction when a single raw material – copper or steel for instance – or a single purchased item have an enormous impact on total cost. In the case of metals and other commodities, decisions whether to enter into safe, long term contracts or to engage in spot buys on the open market carry 'make or break' implications for the company's success and they should not be made without senior leadership's clear direction.

31

These issues will be covered more in the execution and metrics sections of the book. The most critical strategic decisions required of senior leadership have to do with the trade-off between price, lead times, and quality.

Many companies have found that it was possible to transition the critical mass of their supplier base to China incrementally – one component at a time – but it is virtually impossible to bring it back in the same manner. As costs in China increase and the hidden costs of an offshore supplier base become more apparent, manufacturers are looking for more domestic sources. While those sources offer superior quality and better lead times, it is difficult to see how a superior supplier translates into actual cost savings sufficient enough to offset higher domestic purchase prices without understanding the role an effective supply chain has in reducing overall costs.

The primary reason for the cost problem is that the cost of offshore sourcing is usually a high fixed cost. Once the company began to source in China with long lead times driving higher inventories and quality concerns increasin, a support infrastructure of inspectors, material handlers and physical material handling and storage resources was installed. The benefit of domestic sourcing comes from eliminating that support infrastructure. Bringing one item back is usually not sufficient enough to reduce that fixed infrastructure cost. It requires a strategic decision to bring virtually all of it back. Once that decision has been made, better quality and shorter lead times can be translated into a lower fixed cost base.

The strategic decision senior leadership must make, which will have profound implications on supply chain structure and execution, is their broad global sourcing strategy. They must provide direction to the supply chain managers concerning the amount of supply that can come from various geographic regions. If sourcing personnel are cut loose to scour the globe in search of the lowest purchase prices, the company will inevitably incur greater inventories as a result of long transit lead times, and the expense of a more substantial supply chain support infrastructure. On the other hand, if sourcing personnel are directed to source the bulk of purchased items within the region that the factory operates, lead times and inventories will be much lower, the support infrastructure will be much smaller, and it will be easier to attain higher quality levels. The trade-off will almost certainly be higher purchase prices.

This trade-off between higher variable costs against lower inventories and fixed costs is a vital senior management decision. It is a major driver of cash flow, profitability, how leveraged the business is in terms of setting the break-even points, and its ability to respond to unexpected changes in the volume and mix of customer demand.

This is hardly the sort of thing that should be determined on an item by item basis at the middle and lower levels of the organization without regard to the overall impact. Yet this is precisely what happens in many organizations. The overall capability of the supply chain was not set on a strategic basis. Rather, it was set by default as the sum of many decisions made one item and one supplier at a time by well-intentioned people in the organization who were making decisions in a vacuum that affect the very security and health of the business.

The corollary to this is the establishment of supply chain performance metrics to assure the supply chain is functioning in support of strategy. In the final section of the book we will explore both financial and non-financial metrics and controls in depth. For senior management it is important to follow through with measures that not only provide necessary control but also re-enforce the strategy. In far too many companies the underlying reason for high inventories and supply chain costs, as well as ongoing supplier quality struggles, is the dominance of purchase price variances in purchasing performance metrics.

It should come as little surprise that, when people are under constant pressure to find ever lower prices, but not under comparable pressure to achieve shorter lead times, or better supplier delivery performance, or improved supplier quality, that they compromise those issues for the sake of price. As one buyer recently said, "*I have been singled out by higher management for praise many times for getting lower prices, but never in my twelve year career has anyone praised or rewarded me for reducing inventory*". When that is the case, the supply chain will be unlikely to support an aggressive market strategy in any meaningful way.

To summarize the supplier strategy decisions incumbent on senior management to make: first they should be heavily involved in identifying critical materials and components in terms of technology and price, as well as broadening the discussion well beyond just purchase price but instead to selecting the best partners for the long term. Second, they should set policy for purchasing objectives for commodities and major investments in raw materials.

Finally, they should decide the nature of the overall makeup of the supplier base. Rightly or wrongly (and most often wrongly) many senior executives and even boards of directors in recent years have set policies for purchasing people to establish a minimum level of China content – 'At least X% of our total buy must come from China'. Such policies provide clear and necessary direction to purchasing. Unfortunately, many such policies were a mistake in hindsight; however, they assured that the supply chain was constructed in support of strategy. Far better to set maximum policies – 'No more than X% of total sourcing should originate in China, and no more than Y% from Mexico, etc… and none of those components can include components A, B or C'. Then, of course, senior management should follow up with a set of controls and metrics to gauge the execution of the supply chain to assure the objectives aimed at impacting cash, profits, and leverage are met.

Chapter 6
Product and Component Proliferation Strategies

No matter what the business model may be, the supply chain performs best when it flows from a high volume of a few input items to smaller volumes of a wide range of output produced from those few inputs:

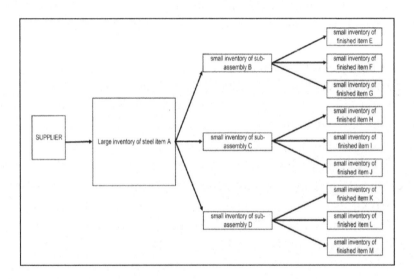

In their heady days, when Motorola was developing Six Sigma and they ruled the electronic manufacturing world they integrated supply chain strategy with product development in a manner rarely seen before. In addition to setting the usual goals for a new product – its features and capabilities, along with total cost – they set very specific supply chain goals … no more than X number of components, no more than Y could be new item numbers and the rest had to use existing part numbers, no more than Z from new suppliers. Their objective was to maximize the flow of the supply chain by minimizing the number of variables the supply chain had to manage and control.

Many companies follow similar approaches today, but most do not. A fundamental principle is that manufacturing, in general, and the supply chain, in particular, abhors change. New items, new suppliers, discontinued items, changes in bills of material and in item number specifications all create change that add cost, disrupt flow and create opportunities for errors. The best flow and best cost come from simplicity.

Of course the primary objective of new product development must be to create products that meet customer requirements, and this consideration must trump supply chain considerations, but the supply chain should not be ignored either and there is often a high price to pay for focusing on part and product direct costs at the exclusion of the supply chain.

A case in point is a manufacturer that produces electro-mechanical devices for the consumer market. After years of looking only to direct cost they woke up one day to the realization that they had 98 variations of the power cords used to plug their products into the wall. It was the culmination of years of developing new products and, when the standard 4' black, flat cord cost 34¢ and someone in marketing found that a red cord would only cost 36¢ the additional 2¢ seemed well worth it to create another point of distinction in the product. The color of the cord really had little or no bearing on how much value a customer would perceive in the product. It was just nice to have and an additional 2¢ on a $10 product seemed trivial.

As is almost always the case, of the 98 variations on power cords, only 15 or so of them were sold in significant volumes, with the rest falling into low volume, sporadic use. The result was a high inventory turnover of the 15 cords purchased from a Chinese source, while the other 83 turned over very slowly, consuming substantial warehouse space, and quite a bit of time to order, receive, cycle count and generally support. All of this affected supply chain cost and added to non-value adding overhead expense; and all of which was largely unnecessary.

Variation in products should always come as far down the manufacturing process as possible. The product development strategy should be based on a few common platforms, to the extent possible, that branch out into a number of different variations in final assembly or toward the end of the production process.

The role of senior management is to develop and communicate a clear strategy for product development that is intelligently integrated with the supply chain. Characteristics of such a vision include:

1. Identification of the basic common platforms upon which new products should be built.
2. Identification of the basic parts or commodities that go into those basic platforms and direction to sourcing personnel to seek out and develop suppliers that can meet future demands for those items and materials in a cost effective manner.
3. Identification of the technical components that create critical points of differentiation, and direction to both engineering and sourcing personnel to identify and develop relationships with sources of supply that can not only provide technical components needed today, but have the ability to provide additional technical components that will be needed in the future products that will be built from the same platforms. Note that there are few practices more destructive to supply chain performance than to have engineers design around components found in a catalogue that meet technical specifications, without regard to the broader ability of the provider of those components to support the volume, lead time, and quality requirements needed for the supply chain to function effectively.
4. The implementation of new product review processes that tolerate – even encourage – proliferation toward the end of the process that make products more useful and appealing to customers, but include rigorous review of any product feature that requires the creation of new basic platforms, or significant variations from existing platforms.
5. Putting in place processes that compel *both* supply chain and engineering personnel to sign off on the addition of any new suppliers.

Chapter 7
Ethical & Social Considerations

It is up to leadership to determine to what degree the supply chain will support the ethical and social values of the organization. There are very real human implications to the company's practices regarding supplier stability – or lack of it, and to global sourcing, just as there are options and implications to the company's policies regarding supplier's use of illegal immigrants.

Manufacturing in countries such as China and Vietnam is governed by a different set of rules regarding worker health and safety, environmental regulations, hourly pay and overtime. In many low cost countries bribery is a cultural norm and it is often unintentionally practiced in developed countries. Practices considered unethical and often illegal in the United States, Canada, Australia and Western Europe are routine in some third world countries.

While it is not our place to dictate the ethical standards a company should put in place, it is important for senior management to set in place clear guidelines for supply chain – especially sourcing – personnel.

At the most common and basic level is the need for a policy concerning the acceptance of gifts and gratuities from suppliers. Best practices typically preclude the acceptance of them. Your buyers pay for their own meals and do not accept gifts from suppliers or potential suppliers. The primary reason for this is not because your sourcing personnel will compromise a sourcing decision for the price of a free lunch so much as it is that, over time, the routine acceptance of such things creates an unhealthy dependence on suppliers for what is often a creeping increase in gratuities. More problematic is the appearance and a negative impact on company morale. Why should someone whose job happens to put them in a sourcing role be entitled to a steady stream of free meals, ballgame tickets and small gifts when an equally diligent and hard-working employee in accounting does not receive similar perks? The best approach is usually a clearly stated zero tolerance policy, and any unsolicited gifts from suppliers that are sent should be put into a common pool and given away or auctioned off at the company picnic or Christmas party. Such an approach eliminates any chance of buyers being unduly influenced or even giving the appearance of being influenced.

More serious is the company's policy governing the need for performing due diligence regarding supplier practices in the areas of supplier treatment of workers and supplier environmental practices. Again, the best companies have comprehensive policies to perform screening, research and inspections to the extent possible to assure that they are not sourcing from 'sweatshops' or companies that blatantly abuse the environment. They do so simply for the sake of feeling a sense of social responsibility. Such practices are often not required, however, and it is up to senior management to determine what the policy will be.

In considering the issue leadership should take into consideration the impact adverse publicity can have should abusive practices at critical suppliers be uncovered and aired by any number of human rights and environmental compliance organizations. While such adverse publicity may not directly hurt the manufacturer much, it can potentially cause damage to the manufacturer's customers. The cost of harming a customer is never worth the financial gain that may appear to arise from looking the other way for unethical suppliers.

Similarly, senior management should consider a policy on supplier use of illegal immigrants. Regardless of the manufacturer's position on the issue, the negative effects of having it come to light that a company did not do at least perfunctory screening to assure that suppliers comply with the law can be devastating. Often having suppliers file certifications that they comply with such laws is enough, but a policy should be in place.

When problems arise in this area it is rarely due to apathy on the part of senior management regarding the company's ethical and social values. More often it is the result of sourcing personnel not having a clear understanding of leadership's position. What may seem obvious and a matter of common sense to the executive may not be so obvious to a buyer tasked with obtaining the best prices.

Another area of common concern is the degree to which any given supplier is dependent on the manufacturer for its business. If, for example, more than half of a supplier's sales are to your company, you may have unintentionally taken on a heavy burden of responsibility for that supplier. If your company were to discontinue the item which that supplier supports, or choose to switch suppliers, your decisions could easily bankrupt the supplier. Many companies have policies in place to assure they are in their suppliers' 'sweet spot', generally viewed as 5-15% of a supplier's sales. In this range the manufacturer is a large enough share of the supplier's business to assure the supplier's full attention and best efforts, but not so large as to create a social dependency when things change.

This is not to say that a manufacturer should never be the lion's share of a supplier's business. There are certainly benefits to such a relationship. It is to point out the dangers of unknowingly being in such a position, and to warn the manufacturer that there are potentially adverse consequences to both the manufacturer and the supplier of such a disproportionate relationship when it is not a thoroughly developed long term partnership.

The final and perhaps most compelling reason for establishing a set of comprehensive social and ethical policies is that even though your current customers may not require you to certify that you have a formal policy, it is becoming more and more common for customers to do so. Without such a policy you may easily find yourself either denied a sales opportunity, or in a position of having to evaluate and restructure your supplier base in a big hurry in order to comply with the requirements of a new customer.

Such a policy, or set of policies, need not be overly detailed or complicated. It is often a simple set of statements accompanied by a certification requirement to be submitted by potential new suppliers, along with a very cursory due diligence requirement for your personnel to follow when they visit suppliers. In the end, it is up to your suppliers to comply, and it is up to you to put in the basic effort and apply basic common sense to weed out any irresponsible suppliers.

Chapter 8
Economic Considerations

Harry Moser, the driver of the Reshoring Initiative, put together what he calls the Total Cost of Ownership Estimator that serves as a very comprehensive tool for evaluating the overall economics of the supply chain. The following is a basic version of the model:

```
CoGS (Cost of Goods Sold)
                          FOB price
                          Packaging
                           Duty
                           Fees
                    Consolidation services
          Routine surface freight, excluding local
            Routine air freight, excluding local
Other Hard Costs
    Carrying cost for intransit offshored product if paid before shipment
              Carrying cost for inventory on-site
                     Prototype cost
                    End-of-life inventory
                     Travel: start-up
                   Travel: audit/maintain
              Pick/place into local inventory
              Purchasing cost, excluding travel
Risk
                   Emergency air freight
                     Rework/quality
           Product liability non-recovery risk
                        IP risk
    Opportunity cost: lost orders, slow response, lost customers
              Economic stability of the supplier
               Political stability of the country
Strategic
         Impact on innovation of distance from mfg. to R&D
       Impact on product differentiation / mass customization
Other
                      Production
                       Shipping
                   Local warehouse
                        Travel
              Disposal of obsolete inventory
```

As you can see, some of the costs in Moser's 'Total Cost' are straightforward, hard costs, while others are necessarily estimates. Whether the manufacturer uses the Total Cost of Ownership Estimator or some other device it is important to consider all of the elements of the model in assessing the economies of the supply chain. The challenge is in how to deal with the soft costs, such as those related to risk; or how to put a value on the impact the distance between manufacturing and R&D will have on innovation.

It is important for the senior leadership to keep in mind the fact that those costs are every bit as real as the differences in purchase prices. What makes them different is that accounting does not know how to put a clear number on them. The tendency is to ignore such costs, or to minimize them in decision making – elevating the importance of those costs that can be accurately determined. However, if senior leadership does not step in and place a value on such things in all probability no one else will,

A very real example is a company that has a plant in China and a plant in the United States. Their business is very good and they need additional capacity. They have been considering expanding their operation in China versus expanding in the United States. Recently a third option has been proposed – to build the new plant in Vietnam. Taking only the clearly known current costs of labor, materials and operating overheads into account the decision should be simple. Vietnam is the lowest cost, followed closely by China, with the USA a distant third. However, it is not that simple.

The problem with China is that China has been managing its currency exchange rate making its costs artificially low. While this has worked to the company's advantage for several years it has created long term problems in China (contributing to inflation and driving labor costs up) and it is a hot political issue in the United States and around the world. In response to pressure from various entities, to stave off the possibility of retaliatory measures from the US government, and to get inflation under control, China has been steadily strengthening its currency. The impact, between inflation driven increases in Chinese labor costs and China easing its currency control, has been an increase in costs of 15%+ for the last few years. Will that continue? If so, for how long?

Vietnam has similar issues. It is the low cost option today, but it has the highest inflation rate in Asia, running anywhere from 12-18% over the last few years. Furthermore, a number of credible organizations that look at various elements of countries' business cultures give Vietnam very low marks. At the time of this writing, Transparency.org ranks Vietnam

112th out of 143 countries in its corruption index. The World Bank ranks Vietnam 98th among countries in its Ease of Doing Business index – worse than China and the country has had a number of bad experiences with the legal and financial infrastructure during its time in China. Indications are that Vietnam will be as bad or worse. The annual study conducted by Carleton University and the Canadian government ranks Vietnam among the world's worst in terms of human rights, and Yale University gives them very poor marks for Environmental health. Finally the World Bank ranks Vietnam poorly in its Logistics Performance Index, and sailing times from Vietnam to the Unites States will be 10% longer than from China, if not more.

The United States, on the other hand, has none of these issues, but the known labor and overhead costs will be substantially higher. There is a large body of anecdotal information from companies that have had the best results from returning from China to the United States, but there is no clear way of knowing whether the results those companies have realized will be the same for the manufacturer in question. So what is the company to do? Compounding the difficulty in answering the question is that it is not enough to place a value on these matters today. The real issue is their effect in the future, which makes already fuzzy economic matters even fuzzier.

These are critical financial decisions that must be made with uncertain information – and no way to make that information certain. It would make for a great business school case study, but this is not business school. It is very real and major decisions must be made that will define the company's supply chain, and in all likelihood, its future.

While everyone would like perfect data – having it would make decision making and strategy issues simple and risk free – the harsh reality is that perfect data does not exist. Senior leadership, and senior leadership alone, must make these fundamental decisions about the supply chain strategy.

Most companies do not face such major, global choices. More often the decisions are smaller in scope. Do we keep the current supplier or switch to a lower cost, but unknown entity that is further away from us? The issues are similar, however.

Chapter 9
Execution Considerations

For most companies the question of how best to execute their supply chain strategy revolves around two fundamental questions: How much of the execution should be computer software driven; and what elements of supply chain execution, if any, should be outsourced?

The software question often boils down to the use of ERP systems. ERP systems are very complicated and very comprehensive software packages that facilitate the planning and execution of the entire supply chain at a very detailed level. In many companies the supply chain strategy and its execution are determined not by management policy or in support of company strategy, but rather by the rules and logic of their ERP system. This is most apparent in the disconnection often seen in companies that have a stated strategy to become a Lean manufacturer, a cornerstone of which is demand pull supply chain execution, yet run the business on a day to day basis with the use of an ERP system constructed to facilitate forecast push supply chain execution.

In Chapter I we referred to the supply chain system as a mysterious, impenetrable 'black box' that limited strategy, rather than

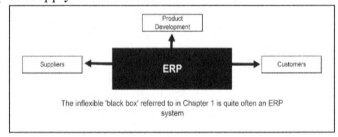

The inflexible 'black box' referred to in Chapter 1 is quite often an ERP system

enhanced it. Quite often that 'black box' is an ERP system that drives execution not as senior management would like it to, but in the manner the developers of the software decided was the best way to manage the business.

Regardless of whether the company has an existing software system, or they are contemplating the acquisition of a new one, it is essential that strategy comes first while software comes second and in a manner that supports the strategy. When management does not establish clear direction concerning how the supply chain should be executed it leaves a vacuum that the software designers are only too happy to fill.

The training that routinely comes with the acquisition of an ERP system is not just training regarding what tab to click to navigate from one screen to another. It is training on what to make and what to buy, when to make it and in what quantities. It is training people to make the fundamental decisions that drive cash flow, inventory levels, and the resulting ability to deliver according to customer requirements (or not).

Leaders must be very clear when it comes to their expectations as to how the supply chain will be executed in support of strategy outside of the software realm. Then they must task their supply chain and IT personnel with the responsibility of assuring that the software tools support that direction. This may mean modifying existing software, or possibly acquiring new software. To blindly assume that an ERP system does what senior management wants it to do in support of the business strategy is a serious mistake. It is not a coincidence that, in most companies, the supply chain and accounting staff are the most adept people in the organization in the use of tools such as Excel spreadsheets. This reflects the reality that the ERP system they work with does not always facilitate the way they have been tasked to run the business. They are compelled to pull data from the ERP system into their spreadsheets in order to use it the way they need to, rather than in the manner the software was designed to be used.

The other major execution concern – that of the use of third party supply chain support services – is similar, although it includes key elements of the make versus buy issue discussed in Chapters 3 and 4.

Most often the use of third parties is in the areas of freight management and remote warehousing and distribution – elements of the supply chain that (1.) involve specialized knowledge; and (2.) are geographically remote from the primary facilities. The use of specialized support services is often a very effective approach, but once again, it is critical that such services support the execution of the strategy set by management. Quite often these functions are treated as almost stand alone operations to be optimized in their own right, and the management of them, including policy and strategy setting, is aimed at optimizing them on their own without regard to how optimizing freight or warehouse efficiency may be sub-optimizing other connected areas of the supply chain.

An example of the right and wrong ways to use outside services can be seen in the comparison between a consumer products company in the western Unites States, and a hardware manufacturer in the Midwest. The consumer products company sells a high volume of products to individuals who order from the company's web site, as well as small quantities to a wide range of small retailers. Because the company is located in Montana and the bulk of the population in the United States is east of the Mississippi River, this results in a high volume of small packages going a long distance individually. FedEx was only too happy to offer them discounted rates and to put their shipping and labeling hardware and software in their facility.

The hardware company has a similar logistics challenge. They sell small quantities in small packages to a wide range of customers scattered throughout the United States. Their approach is much different, however. They have analyzed their customer locations within the various UPS zones, and have contracted with both UPS and a variety of trucking firms. They bundle up all of the small packages going to each zone and ship them by common carrier to a UPS facility within the zone. UPS then delivers them at their lowest rates because the packages do not cross from one zone to another (which would trigger higher rates). The overall cost of shipping for the hardware company is much lower than that of the consumer products company.

The consumer products company has essentially delegated their distribution and logistics strategy to FedEx, which optimizes it for the benefit of both companies but primarily FedEx, of course. The hardware company, on the other hand, has carefully thought through their logistics strategy and uses UPS and the truckers to execute a strategy of the hardware company's design.

The point is that senior management should think their way through the supply chain execution as if they were operating it entirely on their own, devising processes that optimize the whole rather than any single element. If it then makes sense to contract some portion of the execution out to a third party, then so be it. But that third party is executing their portion of the supply chain in support of overall company goals instead of as an independent entity.

The most common shortcoming in this area tends to be freight. Quantities of inbound materials are often maximized in order to minimize freight costs. While this is certainly a worthwhile objective, it often drives excess inventory into the factory or distribution center. The dollar saved in freight cost is often more than offset by two dollars of excess cost resulting from the unnecessary inventory storage, handling and management costs.

Whether it is a computer system or the use of third party service providers, the role of senior leadership is the same. The manner in which the supply chain should be executed must be determined by senior leadership taking the entire supply chain into consideration and assuring that the processes clearly support the broader strategic objectives of the business. Only when this execution strategy has been developed should portions of it be relegated to software tools and third party service providers.

Chapter 10
Supply Chain Risk Considerations

The issue of risk has been cited a number of times in this section and it is a very important element of consideration in leadership's role in setting the company's supply chain strategy. There is no way to avoid some degree of risk, and there is no magic formula to mitigate it. In many regards though, risk mitigation comes down to common sense.

Supply chain risk can be broken down into three basic levels: Country risk, regional risk, and individual supplier risk. Senior leadership should establish a basic process for determining and monitoring supply chain risk at each level.

Country risk includes such matters as the political and economic stability of the country in which suppliers are located. Specifically is gets at matters such as the possibility of revolution, currency collapse or some other major news-making event that could put the supplier in peril. A disappointing number of senior leaders do not take the time to keep up with the news in the countries they depend on for supply. This cannot be the case. Managing the risk begins with knowing where the supply chain is – this includes not just the firm's direct suppliers but the location of the suppliers' suppliers. It is then a simple matter of learning about the government and the economy and keeping up with the news.

As stated previously, the company should set in place policies to limit exposure in any country that is even somewhat risky. A specific risk assessment process should then be established, consisting of little more than regularly scheduled meetings between the company's key personnel to discuss the current risk level in countries from which they source – China, Mexico, Vietnam, India, etc… - and either confirm or modify the policy regarding how much they are willing to source in that country.

Regional risk is slightly different in that includes such issues as weather and logistical infrastructure. How prone is the region to weather related catastrophes or earthquakes? Are there any logistical bottlenecks? One port, one bridge, one major highway? This is more of a one-time assessment that should be part of the initial supplier assessment. Senior leadership should assure that a process is in place to evaluate this type of risk in the initial supplier selection process. You don't want to learn that there is only one bridge going in and out of a key supplier's facility after that bridge has collapsed.

Finally, and most common, is individual company risk. There is always risk of fire, strikes, insolvency and a number of other things that can happen at the company level. This sort of risk is best managed with an ongoing due diligence process. There should be policies and processes in place to assure that each supplier routinely conducts and passes fire inspections; that the supplier's financial results are reviewed and that sufficient liquidity is there, that labor contracts are well known and the manufacturer is well informed of any looming contract talks or other issues that could result in a work stoppage.

For the most part this aspect of risk can be delegated to the supplier itself. Suppliers should be required to submit their risk mitigation strategy. What is their back-up plan in the event of fire or tornado? Do they have other facilities capable of stepping in and meeting your requirements, or partnerships with other firms that can fill the void?

In the end risk is an unavoidable aspect of business and the supply chain will always be prone to a degree of risk. The least acceptable risk is the one you never thought of. The obligation of senior management is to put in place basic processes to assure that all reasonable risks are identified, evaluated, considered and continually monitored. The diligence of the assessment and monitoring is in direct proportion to the magnitude of the risk. If you opt to buy from a supplier whose plant is located directly on the shores of the Gulf of Mexico, be sure there is a back-up plan in the event of a hurricane, and that someone in sourcing is keeping an eye on the weather in the Gulf as storms develop during hurricane season. It is that simple and there is no need to belabor the point. Management shouldn't put itself in a position of being caught totally by surprise, having never considered the possibility of a storm affecting your supply chain.

Chapter 11
The Rapidly Changing Core Structure of Supply Chains

Recent years have seen the beginning of a radical change in supply chains brought about by four convergent factors:

1. The proliferation of access to and comfort with the Internet
2. The emergence of secure payment processes over the Internet
3. The radical improvement in small package delivery reliability and cost due to the fierce competition between FedEx, UPS, the US Postal Service, and others.
4. Widespread adaptation of Lean Manufacturing practices that enable manufacturers to produce in smaller batches without cost degradation.

Individually and together they have driven the elimination of entire, significant segments of supply chains that added cost but typically added little or no value.

The examples that emerged first and for obvious reasons were those related to sensory media products – music, movies, and books. Video rental stores, retailers of CD's, book stores and others were no longer needed as the product could be purchased and electronically delivered directly to the end customer. The traditional supply chain activities of converting the media to physical carriers (discs and paper) along with all of the packaging, warehousing, delivery and many of the brick and mortar retailing were rendered unnecessary. From Border's Bookstores to Blockbuster Video hundreds (if not thousands) of businesses became obsolete and went under.

The phenomena was not limited to media products that could be delivered electronically. Amazon has decimated brick and mortar retailing by essentially selling online directly from the distribution center. More recently products from razors sold by The Dollar Shave Club to automobiles sold by Tesla are available via the Internet without the need for packaging, distribution centers, dealers and retailers. There is a growing number of manufacturers selling directly via the Internet, cutting out the cost of whole supply chain segments that added costs but not value for the end customers.

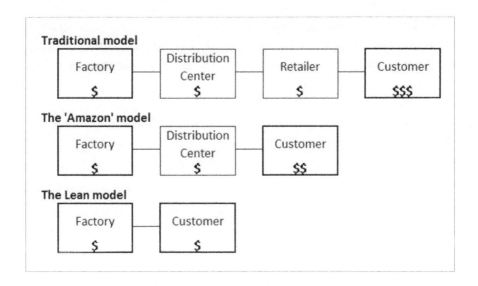

Increasingly, end users of products can make repairs, install products, and perform improvements with knowledge from YouTube and parts they purchased online. The net result of this trend is that smaller producers have access to markets that were traditionally cost prohibitive for them to enter. From the customer's perspective, they have access to a much wider range of product offerings at a lower price as the non-value adding waste of the traditional supply chain models has been eliminated.

Many businesses that did not add much value but were necessary in former days are finding that these changes in technology, production, and delivery have eliminated that necessity; and exposed the lack of value they created.

This trend will not slow down. It is vitally incumbent upon the leadership of every manufacturer to be keenly aware of the supply chain – both upstream and downstream, and to know the links that add cost without adding corresponding value. It must be assumed that those links will go the way of Blockbuster sooner, rather than later. And leadership must have a strategy to succeed in the rapidly emerging world in which such links are no longer there.

Assuming that any particular company or its supply chain is exempt from this shift in business is highly dangerous. Far better to assume that, as you read this, some very creative people are hard at work in bringing changes such as these to your industry and its supply chains.

The better strategy is the proactive one, and one that sees opportunity. The opportunity is particularly ripe for the smaller producers. Not long ago Amazon was a small start-up and now they are slowly slaying the giant, Walmart. Dollar Shave Club began with a shoestring operation and a home-grown YouTube video and is now wreaking havoc on the likes of Procter & Gamble.

SECTION II
Techniques and Principles

There are a number of techniques, technologies and guiding principles to supply chain management that have evolved over the years. In general, the trend in the latter half of the twentieth century was to more and more complicated MRP logic in large scale computer applications. More recently the trend has been towards more simple, more visually and manually controlled demand pull approaches as Lean Manufacturing principles have become more widely adopted.

Most organizations find there is no one generic approach that fits their business and the company strategy perfectly, and they use a combination of techniques. In this section we will describe MRP logic (the standard supply chain logic embedded in ERP systems) as well as demand pull, or Lean, supply chain principles. A third body of thought – the Theory of Constraints – is also described since it is an essential principle to the design and management of any supply chain.

We will also discuss the basic principles of lead times, variation in demand patterns, and lot sizing. These are the basic factors driving the flow and economy of the supply chain.

It is important for the supply chain professional to have a thorough understanding of the basic driving forces of supply chain performance, as well as the basic options at hand for designing the supply chain architecture. The next section will take these building blocks and describe how they should be considered and put into practice in a manner that best supports the company's strategy.

CHAPTER 12
Planning and Forecasting

Peter Drucker, the great management thinker, once described a hard-learned lesson from a forecasting failure as proceeding, *"from a self-evident assumption by means of impeccable mathematics to an asinine conclusion."* He wrote, *"We must start out with the premise that forecasting is not a respectable human activity and not worthwhile beyond the shortest of periods."*[i]

"The question that faces the strategic decision-maker is not what his organization should do tomorrow. It is, 'What do we have to do today to be ready for an uncertain tomorrow?' The question is not what will happen in the future. It is, 'What futurity do we have to build into our present thinking and doing, what time spans do we have to consider, and how do we use this information to make a rational decision now?'"

For all practical purposes, he was talking about lead times and their relationship to strategy. In far too many companies, planned strategies are undermined by excessive lead times and supply chain execution is undermined by impractical strategies.

The best example of this strategy-supply chain disconnect is in the retail industry when planning for holiday sales. The December holidays are usually the most critical period of the year for retailers, often generating almost half of their annual sales and profits for the entire year in a compressed six week or less selling period. As retailers have shifted their sourcing from domestic suppliers to foreign ones – again, most often in China – they have radically extended their lead times. The surge in buying also creates capacity problems for suppliers, shipping companies and ports, further extending the lead times. As a result, in order to have merchandise in stock by November, product must be shipped from China by the end of September. In order to ship by September, retail orders must be placed with Chinese suppliers by early August and often sooner than that.

This puts retailers in the difficult position of having to project in June or July what consumers will want six months later. Predicting what will be in demand is always a difficult task in light of changing consumer trends and desires. In times of economic uncertainty it is made even more challenging by the fact that overall volumes are highly unknown, let alone the mix of products within the total demand.

To the degree that the predictions of future customer demands are wrong, two things happen and neither is good: Let's say the forecast is based on an assumption that consumers will want an equal mix of red product and blue product. When the holiday buying season arrives, however, it turns out the customers strongly prefer red over blue. The retailer will either miss sales due to having an insufficient stock of red items, or incur substantial expediting costs by bringing more red products in from China at the last minute via air freight. At the same time, the retailer is left with an excess of blue products in inventory when the holiday shopping season ends. In light of weak customer demand for the blue products, the retailer is faced with having to offer significant price reductions and stage 'clearance sales' in the months following the holidays to sell off the excess inventory.

There is a direct correlation between the accuracy of a forecast and the level of detail to be forecasted, as well as, between the accuracy of a forecast and the distance into the future that must be forecasted. The weather is a good example.

Even in June you can forecast with a high degree of accuracy that the weather in Chicago probably will be very cold next January. However, it is impossible to forecast with any confidence at all what the temperature will be at Daly Plaza at 2:45 PM next January 16th.

The gap between strategy and forecasting follows this logic. The strategy the company would like to pursue is typically expressed in broader business terms. For example, the retailer plans to increase market share by X% and profits by Y% by positioning itself as the store with the broadest selection, outstanding customer service, shortest check-out lines, and best overall customer service in the area, and to do so with prices slightly higher but still generally competitive with the other retailers in the area.

The supply chain, however, needs very specific input. "Broadest selection" is not nearly specific enough. It needs to know precisely how many of Item A and how many of Item B to order now – in July – in order to achieve those goals.

Inevitably, the actual strategy of the company will be to react to forecast error with a last minute advertising campaign attempting to sway customers away from the red products and to the blue ones, re-arranging the store layout to display the blue products more prominently, and offering slight discounts on blue products in December in order to avoid having to offer deep discounts in January. In short, the execution will be in response to forecast error and supply chain realities, rather than in support of the original, broad strategic plan which management put in place.

The key point is that forecasting is inherently inaccurate to a degree that directly correlates with the length of time and level of detail to be forecasted – which means the lead time. It is essential that the company strategy take this into account. As Drucker said, the question to ask is, *"What futurity do we have to build into our present thinking and doing, what time spans do we have to consider, and how do we use this information to make a rational decision now?"* In other words, how does the inevitable error in forecasting impact our ability to execute the strategy?

The hypothetical retailer in our discussion sourced from China to realize low prices, but had to accept long lead times as a result. Those long lead times resulted in undermining the ability to execute the basic strategy. In order to execute the strategy the retailer would have been better off had it sourced from a domestic supplier with shorter lead times, even if it meant paying slightly higher price for the merchandise.

This is not to suggest that shorter lead times and low prices are incompatible – that there is an unavoidable trade-off between lead times and prices. That is not the case, especially in the era of Lean Manufacturing in which many manufacturers are applying Lean principles and realizing simultaneous cost and lead time reductions. Rather, it is to explain the need to set firm priorities for the architects of the supply chain. If the strategy is based on superior customer service and selection, the direction senior management should set for the supply chain is that low lead times are critical, and that supply chain management should seek to find the lowest prices among the short lead time supplier alternatives. On the other hand, if the strategy is to compete on the basis of price, the direction to supply chain decision makers should be to negotiate the best lead times among the low price supply alternatives. In other words, if short lead times are essential to execution of the strategy then supply chain people must assure short lead times even if that means higher purchase prices. Or if low prices are the cornerstone of strategy, then sourcing people must know that negotiating low prices is paramount, even if that entails long lead times. Ideally, of course, they can get both.

It is the lack of direction to supply chain decision makers – or more often, conflicting direction – that causes many companies to get into trouble. While the strategy may call for the supremacy of short lead times and responsiveness, the performance measurements set in place for supply chain execution are often centered on purchase price. They operate under the reasonable assumption that purchase price is always the highest priority because that is the critical measure of their performance. They fail to adjust the supply chain priorities because senior management has failed to adjust the direction they are provided by changing the formal processes for measuring supply chain success.

The supply chain priorities are rarely of a company-wide "one size fits all" nature. The strategies and priorities often differ between the various markets, channels and customers the company serves. An excellent example of this, as discussed in Chapter 1, was when John Deere moved into the consumer lawn mower business. Their traditional markets had been the agricultural and commercial sectors, where a wide variety of relatively expensive, relatively low volumes of a wide variety of products were sold. That business required domestic sources because having the ability to procure a wide range of low volume, very high quality components was more important than the purchase prices for those components. Again, it was not that price was unimportant – it was just less important than the responsiveness inherent in a domestic supplier base with its shorter lead times.

When they entered the consumer lawn mower business they were entering a radically different supply chain. By manufacturing and selling to the consumer market, they were in an arena in which very high volumes of a narrow range of products were being sold, and prices were critical. That supply chain lent itself more to an offshore supply base that could meet their price needs better, even though long lead times were inevitable.

The resulting supply chain included both domestic and offshore suppliers for nearly identical components. The commercial products and consumer products were obviously not identical, but the offshore supplier of hoses for the consumer products, for instance, could have easily manufactured the similar hoses for the commercial products; and the domestic supplier of hoses for the commercial products was technically capable of producing the hoses for the consumer products. In this case, however, it made sense to have multiple suppliers for comparable items in order to meet the supply chain requirements necessary to execute Deere's strategy in each of its markets.

Even when there are not multiple markets and multiple strategies, the supply chain priorities are often varied. The underlying principle behind the Deere approach was consideration for the consequences of inevitable forecast error – Drucker's *"what time spans do we have to consider, and how do we use this information to make a rational decision now?"*

The consumer products were low variation and high volume, so the company could afford to carry excess inventory to buffer against forecast errors while secure in the knowledge that volumes were high enough that any excess inventory could be sold in fairly short order. On the other hand, any excess inventory of components for the commercial products would be much more difficult to sell in light of the wide range of products and comparatively uneven and low volume demand. The inventory risk was much higher for commercial products inventory than it was for consumer products.

While the degree of forecast error is the same, the consequences of error are in direct relation to the consistency of demand. While Walmart may sell more office supplies such as pens and staplers over the holiday season, they sell them year round so there is little risk of carrying excess inventory to protect the uncertainty of how many of each type of pen and stapler they will sell in December. On the other hand, any Christmas decorations remaining after December will not sell for a long time and will have to be sold at substantially lower prices – often at a loss.

In summary, senior management must recognize that strategy and forecasting both concern the future. Strategy is basically a statement of what the company *would like to do, or what they need to do* in the future. Forecasting, on the other hand, attempts to express what the *company will do* in the future in a very detailed manner. These endeavors must be connected, and in a manner that recognizes the inherent weakness in forecasting. What the company can produce and can sell is a function of lead times, and the inventory decisions made to buffer against forecast error. To the extent that strategy is based on assumptions of the products available to make and sell in the future, the success of the strategy is wholly dependent on the formal direction flowing from strategy to supply chain architects to decision makers.

CHAPTER 13
How MRP / ERP Systems Work

The most common formal systems approach to inventory management and supply chain scheduling is the application of Enterprise Resources Planning (ERP) systems, although the deepening understanding of Lean Manufacturing and demand pull is causing many people to rethink some of its basic rules and logic. The function within ERP that handles factory scheduling is MRP – Manufacturing Resources Planning. The terminology and use of acronyms can be a bit confusing, and it is worth a few moments to understand the background of MRP/ERP and what they mean.

The Origin and Principles Behind MRP/ERP

MRP traces its roots back to the early 1960's when a consultant named Oliver "Ollie" Wight developed a computer-based method of planning inventories and scheduling factories for JI Case that he called "material requirements planning" – MRP. At about the same time an IBM engineer named Joe Orlicky was doing the same thing at the Rock Island Arsenal. These systems converted the material needed to produce to a schedule into their detailed requirements, and compared them to available inventory to determine what should be purchased and built – and when to do so. A few years later, comparing the resources needed to build the schedule – machines and people – to available resources was added. This function was known as capacity planning and the acronym 'MRP' changed from denoting 'Material Requirements Planning' to 'Manufacturing Resources Planning'. You might still occasionally hear materials and supply chain managers refer to 'little MRP" and 'big MRP'. Little MRP refers to the specific functionality within the system that converts demand into material requirements, while Big MRP means the broader system that includes capacity planning.

The Evolution from
MRP to ERP

	First MRP systems are developed	APICS emerges as the leader of MRP knowledge base	MRP becomes MRP II with addition of accounting application		MRP II evolves into ERP with the addition of other functional applications	
1960	1970		1980	1990	2000	2010

As the time line above demonstrates, MRP has evolved over the years. In the 1980's MRP became MRPII as cost accounting was integrated with the scheduling and inventory management logic. This was a logical step since inventory transactions are at the heart of traditional manufacturing cost accounting approaches. In many companies, accounting considerations drive how MRP is used on the factory floor to a much greater degree than scheduling needs.

By the 1990's MRPII had further expanded to include a wide range of other related functions, including broader human resource issues and engineering product design schedules, MRPII became known as ERP (Enterprise Resources Planning). It should be noted that a variation on MRP/ERP known as Distribution Requirements Planning (DRP) also exists. It is more akin to early material requirements planning as it performs purchased material and inventory planning, without as much of the manufacturing capacity functionality, and is essentially MRP for distributors.

Beginning with what they the called 'The MRP Crusade' in the early years of MRP with Ollie Wight at the forefront, the American Production and Inventory Control Society (APICS) emerged as the central authority on MRP application and functionality. MRP is extremely complicated and extensive and, over the years, APICS has developed a thorough and accurate body of knowledge on how it should be implemented and effectively applied. The organization runs a certification program and becoming 'APICS Certified' is still a very reliable validation of a thorough understanding of the system.

Over the years APICS has fallen from being the dominant authority on supply chain management, largely due to disagreements within the supply chain management community over MRP's conflicts

61

with some of the Lean Manufacturing principles, to their current less influential role. Those disagreements have revolved around MRP's applicability, however, and there is still no question that APICS remains the primary authority on MRP.

It is important to note that the journey from MRP to ERP has not been an evolution so much as it has been an expansion. As the graphic to the right demonstrates, including accounting applications to MRP in its transition 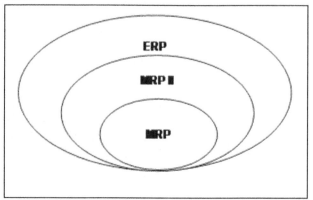 to MRPII, then incorporating other functions in the transition to ERP did not change the original MRP logic, so much as it added to it. If Ollie Wight or Joe Orlicky could see a modern ERP system, while they would be surprised by the inclusion of so many additional business functions, and they would be bowled over by the usability that PC and Windows based technology has added, they would still be quite comfortable with the basic factory scheduling and inventory planning logic. That logic has not changed in any significant manner in the fifty years since they first developed it.

This brief history lesson is important in order to provide the background and context for these systems. They were developed quite a while ago - long before pull planning and Lean were known to American manufacturers. MRP and ERP were not intended to support demand pull. To the extent that the supply chain objectives and strategy of a firm have changed over the decades since MRP and ERP were developed, they may not be the most effective tools to use.

MRP Complexities

MRP is regarded as a 'push system', as opposed to a 'pull system'. The term 'push system' means that material is pushed into the factory based on projected, or forecasted, demand for products. 'Pull systems', on the other hand, pull purchasing and production into and through the factory based on actual customer orders. Pull is a fundamental aspect of

Lean Manufacturing, and we will discuss it in considerable detail in the next chapter. It is important to note, however, that it is only generally accurate to describe MRP as 'push'. While most MRP users drive the system with a combination of actual customer orders and forecasts of future customer requirements, it is possible to drive MRP entirely with actual demand and in some cases manufacturers do this.

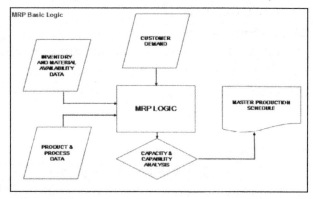

As previously mentioned, MRP is comprehensive and complicated. It entails creating and maintaining an extensive data base of virtually every aspect of the products and the manufacturing processes and capabilities as the figure shows. Production and inventory events must be captured and fed ino the system. The system is designed to continually re-plan and re-optimize production and purchasing plans, so continually knowing what is happening and what is needed are essential elements of MRP. It is best understood by breaking it down into some basic blocks, beginning at the front end with demand and how it is introduced to MRP.

The front end, or demand management end, of MRP is all about lead times. The central concern is the comparison of

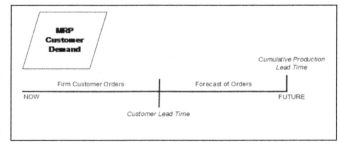

'customer lead times' to 'cumulative production lead times'. The 'customer lead time' is the amount of notice the factory has that a customer order has been received before it must ship. The 'cumulative lead time' is the total time required to procure materials and manufacture the finished product. As we stated, MRP is complicated and the procurement lead time typically includes not only the supplier lead time – how long does it take for your supplier to ship something after you send them a purchase order – but time for all of the related events, as well. These include time to prepare the purchase order, transit time from the supplier to your location, time to receive the material into your inventory, time to perform any necessary quality inspections, and so forth. All of these times must be determined and entered into the MRP system for each item you purchase. The manufacturing lead times include similar details, reflecting the total time needed to go from the realization that something must be produced until it is ready for shipment.

In the rare circumstances in which the cumulative lead times are less than customer lead times – if, say, the customer gives you an order for something to be shipped in four weeks and you are capable of buying all of the materials and making the product in three weeks – no forecast is necessary. (Note that you will still require some statement of forecast demands in order to plan needed capacity, but that will be addressed later). For purposes of procuring material and scheduling the factory it can all be done based on firm customer orders.

It is much more common to have customer orders well within the cumulative production lead times, as shown in the figure above. Say customer orders must be shipped a week after you receive them, while your cumulative production lead times are four weeks. (When a manufacturer is purchasing materials from Asia, or purchasing small quantities of custom made items, the supplier lead times are usually much longer – often measured in months.)

In this case, you need to know what items purchasing must place on order today for receipt in four weeks, even though you only know for certain what your customers want in one week. That is where forecasting comes into play. MRP must know what you want to build over the course of the cumulative lead time, so the known customer orders must be supplemented with a projection of what you assume the orders will look like over the second, third and fourth week out into the future.

Depending on the nature of your business forecasting can range from being fairly easy to nearly impossible. Many manufacturers have items at both extremes, while most find it virtually impossible to forecast anything with much accuracy.

The next chart shows the historical demand pattern for two items. Both average fifty per week. The one on the left has a very stable demand history and is very easy to forecast with a high degree of accuracy. The forecast error rate will be low, and the risk associated with buying parts and building products to the forecast is low since management can have a high degree of confidence that anything put into inventory will soon be sold.

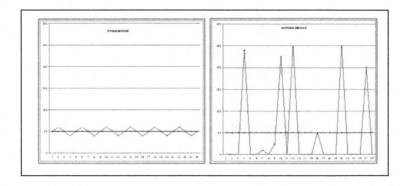

The item on the right, however, is inherently un-forecastable by any statistical means. In supply chain parlance it is known by the unsophisticated term as having 'lumpy demand'. The problem is that by standard regression analysis, demand for the item on the left can be projected to be 50 per week plus or minus 14 with a 98% confidence level. Planning for 64 will enable the supply chain to deliver 98% of the time on-time to customer lead times with relatively little excess inventory. The same mathematical analysis of the item to the right would project 50 per week plus or minus 177 in order to provide the same 98% probability of meeting customer needs.

Keeping an extra 14 items in inventory to meet a peak in customer demand for the item to the left will result in an inventory that turns 28 times annually (50 per week x 52 weeks = 2,600 per year) ÷ (50 per week average + 3x14 = 92) = 28. The "3x14" is the number of unknown weeks multiplied by the maximum potential order quantity of 64 per week. This obviously is excellent turnover and low risk for the manufacturer.

Planning for an extra 177 per week for the item on the right by the same calculation would result in an inventory turning over 4 times, a much less attractive investment.

The problem is that there is simply no way to mathematically project exactly when one of the spikes in demand for the item on the right will occur, or to predict the exact size of the spike. Despite the impossibility of mathematically forecasting items with lumpy, erratic demand, many companies persist in the attempt. The inevitable forecast inaccuracy drives excessive buying and producing of some items and insufficient buying and producing of others. High inventories without adequate on time customer delivery performance are the result.

The only means of predicting the behavior of such items that has any chance of success is customer specific forecasting done manually by the sales people who are in regular contact with the customers buying the items. In other words, having the sales force try to talk to the customers and ask when they expect such orders to be placed, and in what quantities is not helpful. Even that approach tends to be inadequate since often times customers do not really know when their needs will arise.

Most companies operate in between these extremes, with items that are only marginally predictable. In many cases, there is considerable internal friction between sales and supply chain personnel. Supply chain people are frustrated with sales' inability to derive accurate forecasts from their knowledge of and communications with customers; and sales people are equally frustrated with supply chain's inability to predict and have available the items the market needs. The problem is that both sides of the debate are expecting the impossible out of the other.

The need to effectively predict and manage the gap between cumulative lead times and customer lead times and the virtual impossibility of predicting and managing it effectively is the greatest weakness of the MRP driven, "push" approach to supply chain management. The harsh reality is that supply chain managers – and senior management – must accept the fact that the only means of assuring on time customer delivery performance is with substantial safety stocks; the levels of which must be calculated based on the length of the time gap between customer and cumulative production lead times while taking into account the degree of variation in demand and other factors. The method for doing this will be discussed in the chapter regarding inventory management, and elsewhere throughout this book.

In summary, the key point to take away from this section of the MRP discussion is that MRP requires a plan for all of the items the factory will sell over the course of the cumulative – procurement plus production – lead time. MRP will plan all of the details of work to be performed to meet this plan. If an item is not in the plan, MRP will not assure the resources necessary to make it are available. Because MRP drives the factory to produce exactly to the projected demand, how well the factory and the resources spent are aligned with actual customer orders is a direct function of the accuracy of this plan.

The next major element of the MRP system is a necessary record of inventories available now, as well as inventories projected to be available in the future. The overall goal of the MRP system is to assure the right amount of inventory is available to ship when customers require it, and to be able to manufacture the right items at the right time. MRP is essentially just a big inventory planning system.

MRP Effectiveness

In order to do its job effectively MRP requires a complete and highly accurate record of on hand inventories at all times. When it performs its function, MRP will begin with the current inventory of each manufactured and purchased item, add to it the expected results when all of the open purchase and production orders are completed, and subtract from it all of the items needed to fulfill the known customer and open manufacturing orders in order to calculate how much of each item will be available at any point in time to meet the planned future demand.

This process of 'netting' the requirements for each item against the quantity of the item expected to be available as indicated in the following figure is at the heart of MRP. Through the netting of required versus available MRP determines what purchase orders should be placed

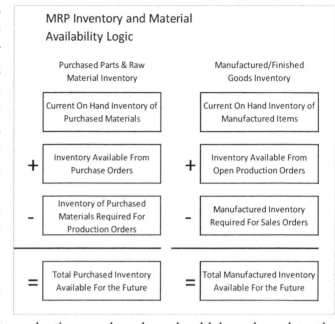

and when, and what production work orders should be released to the factory and when.

Clearly the starting point is an accurate record of current inventories. If the MRP system believes there are 150 of an item on hand when there are really only 100 of them, and the demand for products that need that particular component total 125, MRP will assume there are enough available and will not tell purchasing to buy more. The plant will not be able to meet customer orders even if the forecast is accurate.

Conversely, if MRP believes there are 100 when there are actually 150 in stock and requirements call for 125, MRP will drive purchasing to buy another 25 of them unnecessarily, resulting in excessive inventory levels.

The effectiveness of MRP is in direct correlation to the accuracy of inventory. If the inventory records are only 80% accurate – that is to say that for 20% of the items in inventory the actual quantities are either more or less than the computer records – then 20% of the purchasing and production orders generated by MRP will be inaccurate. They will be driving purchasing and production to buy and build items that are either over or under actual needs, resulting in a combination of missed customer shipments and excessive inventories.

Most MRP authorities will agree that a minimum of 95% inventory accuracy is necessary for MRP to be effective. When inventory levels are substantially below that level the system loses its integrity and breaks down. We will discuss common causes of inventory inaccuracy in later chapters, but in gaining an understanding of the basic functionality of MRP it is important to understand that MRP is absolutely dependent on highly accurate inventory records.

MRP Data Bases & Records

The next major element of an MRP system is a data base of product and process information, telling the system exactly what the products consist of and how they are made. These records include bills of material listing all of the component parts of an end item; item routers that describe the series of steps that go into producing the end item; and information about the resources – both people and equipment – available for production.

The primary, or top, record is some variation on an 'item master file', containing basic information about every item the company makes or buys. In addition to considerable accounting information, the master record will indicate if an item is manufactured or purchased, and if purchased, from whom and what the lead time is. It may also include information that relates to a family of products, and customer information, such as the item number the customer uses to identify it, which is normally a different number than the one the manufacturer uses.

Linked to the master record is the Bill of Material. In MRP, the bills of material are 'indented' to indicate how the various parts come together. The figure below shows a basic bill of material structure. In this case, the product sold to a customer is the Widget 12345-00.

```
12345-00   Widget sold to customer             M
    (1) 23456-01   Widget packing box           P
    (1) 34567-01   Widget sub-assembly A        M
        (1) 45678-01   Widget bracket X         P
        (1) 56789-02   Widget base X            P
        (1) 78912-01   Widget core X            P
        (4) 99900-01   Screws                   P
    (1) 246810-00  Widget instruction book      P
```

In order to make a Widget item #12345-00, a purchased Widget packing box, a manufactured Widget sub-assembly A, and a purchased Widget instruction book have to be put together. Since the Widget sub-assembly A is a manufactured item, another level of the bill of material is necessary to describe what goes into its manufacturing. In this case, a Widget bracket, a Widget base, a Widget core and 4 Screws have to be assembled to make the Widget sub-assembly.

The Role of the BOM

The primary purpose of the Bill of Material (BOM) is to identify all of the items that will be needed in order to have the Widget available to meet the customer orders. Purchasing requirements and production schedules will be derived by multiplying the planned requirements for the Widget by the quantities of each item it takes to make the Widget. BOMs must be comprehensive and accurate, since MRP only knows to plan for the parts that are on the BOMs and in the quantities the BOMs indicate.

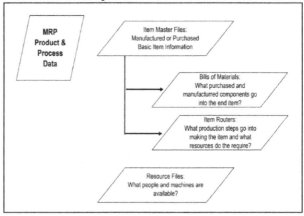

The companion to each BOM is a process routing file, indicating the sequential steps involved in making each manufactured item. In the case of our Widget, its routing file would indicate where the final packing is performed (Packing Station #1, for instance), along with how many hours are required to pack the Widget, and how many people will be working at the operation.

Another routing file would exist for the Widget sub-assembly X that would list its information regarding the steps involved in making the sub-assembly, what machine or assembly station is used, how long it takes and how many people are involved. An important element of the routing files is information concerning lead times. Not only do these files indicate which pieces of equipment must be used to make the products, but how long it will take.

Finally, resource files are essential to MRP, listing the various pieces of equipment, along with their availability in terms of hours per day or week.

Armed with a comprehensive statement of current and future demand, a thorough data base of what parts and processes go into making every product, files of what the company has to work with in terms of existing inventories, purchase orders placed in the past that are due to arrive, and the production resources available, MRP can serve its fundamental purpose – to create 'optimum' production and purchasing plans and schedules.

As the next figure indicates, the heart of MRP logic includes three basic functions. First it 'explodes' the Bill of Material for each end item for which demand exists into requirements for each purchased and manufactured item. In the case of our Widget, if the firm's customer orders and forecast totaled 100 Widgets, it would search down through the BOM and determine that, in order to make 100 of them, 100 packing boxes and instruction books must be on hand, and that production must provide 100 of the Widget sub-assemblies. It will also blow through the sub-assemblies to its purchased components, and determine that 100 brackets, bases, and cores must be made available, along with 400 screws.

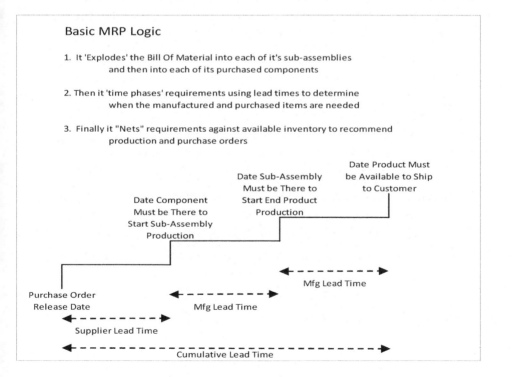

Armed with the total requirement for each component of every end item, MRP will 'net' these gross requirements against the inventories currently on hand and against any purchase orders currently open in order to determine how much of the demand can be met with current stock and parts already in process through production or from suppliers. The gaps will be identified as the net new requirements for purchasing to procure and production to build.

Along the way, MRP is 'time phasing' everything, based on the lead times. Starting with the required date an item is needed to ship to a customer, MRP will work backwards from that date and determine when production must start to build the item to meet that date. Once the production start date is determined, MRP will look at the supplier lead times for each part that production will need, and back up from the production start date to determine when the purchase orders for each component must be placed in order to assure that all of the parts needed will arrive in time for production.

MRP Output & Benefits

The output of the MRP system, then, is a comprehensive plan for producing and purchasing every item, including the dates and quantities needed. This can be done on a 'one for one' basis, but more often manufacturers build standard lot sizes into the system. For instance, our Widget might have gross requirements totaling 112, and there may be 32 Widgets in inventory, leaving a net requirement of 80 to be built in order to meet projected demand. The MRP system may have a production lot size of 25 associated with that Widget, however, indicating that when the factory builds Widgets it does so in quantities of 25 at a time. In that case, MRP would round the 80 to be built up to its next increment of 25 – which would be 100. So the MRP production and purchasing plans would call for 100 Widgets to be built and for the components that build those 100 widgets to be available.

MRP systems also allow for the inclusion of safety stock levels – a quantity of any item management wants to deduct from the on hand inventory quantities that MRP assumes to be available for use. Again looking at our widget, if there are 32 in inventory, with a safety stock level of 30, MRP would assume only 2 of the Widgets in inventory are available to meet the demand of 112, and would generate a net new requirement for purchasing and production of 110 Widgets.

While lot sizing and setting safety stock levels are perhaps the most frequently used adjustments to true requirements in MRP, there are many more detailed features and capabilities within most MRP software packages that enable management, schedulers, and buyers to 'tweak' the system to generate output that is modified to fit how the company wants to execute. While these data fields within MRP provide management with a high degree of control over MRP output, they are quite dangerous. Increasing lot sizes or safety stocks, or over-stating purchasing or production lead times all have the effect of driving more inventory into the company, and they can drive the plant to dedicate more capacity to building inventory. Incidents of abuse of these MRP parameters are frequent and it is not at all uncommon to see factories with excessive inventory levels as a result.

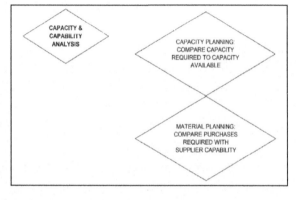

Before the MRP output becomes a firm plan for production and purchasing the system has a capacity and purchasing reality check feature. Referred to as Capacity Planning, as MRP determines the detailed production requirements, and multiplies the times required for each production step by the quantities to be produced and summarizes the time requirements into a total workload for each production resource, then compares it to the time available for each resource. The purpose is to enable management to evaluate the overall MRP plan in terms of its load on capacity. A plan that cannot be met with available capacity would be pointless to attempt to execute.

Capacity planning is simply a review of the gaps between needed capacity and available capacity, providing management with an opportunity to change either the production plan or the available capacity prior to going ahead with MRP's recommendations. While the system enables management to review the workload on every resource, typically management only looks at the overall load on a few machines that are known to be critical capacity bottlenecks, or have special considerations. Management will also look at the overall labor requirement – how many people are needed to perform the labor hours in the MRP plan compared to the current workforce. This broad approach is called 'Rough Cut Capacity Planning', and it is a quick means of looking at the big picture to make sure there are no glaring gaps between what is needed and what is possible.

Similarly, the system identifies problems with supplier lead times. In our Widget example, MRP may generate a net requirement for 50 new Widget cores to be purchased in order to be available for production in one week, based on the forecast and actual orders, and the expected timing of those orders. The Widget core supplier may have a two week lead time, however, indicating that it is not possible to purchase the cores and have them in time to build the Widgets in the time frame that the customer needs. Before locking in on the MRP plan management will want to adjust the schedules if it is impossible to procure materials in time to execute the plan. Again, while MRP generates the data needed to look at every purchased or production item that has a requirement inside the lead time, but usually only the major items are evaluated, or those with substantial gaps. Management trusts that production and purchasing people will work out all of the smaller gaps between material required and material available.

The MRP output may be accepted as is, or management may make changes to the forecast, safety stocks, or other parameters as a result of the gaps and problems found during the review process, and rerun MRP with the new inputs. This iterative process may repeat a number of times until management is satisfied with the plan. The MRP output then becomes the Master Schedule. The Master Schedule typically reflects the production and purchasing plans in somewhat broad, weekly buckets. For each item in the Master Schedule where MRP has created any necessary production or purchase orders on a 'planned' basis – only recommendations are given at that stage. It is up to the buyers and planners in the company to review each item and MRP's recommended or planned orders, and then to create real, or 'firm', work or purchase orders. Along with MRP recommended new orders, MRP recommends changes to existing orders – either to move them in or push them out, or to change the quantities, based on whatever has changed since the last time the MRP system ran and a Master Schedule was created.

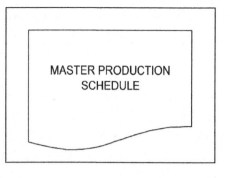

In most companies, running the entire MRP system and creating a Master Schedule occurs weekly, although it can be run more or less frequently if a different timetable makes more sense.

Creating comprehensive MRP generated plans are one thing, but executing them is another matter entirely. Following the creation of MRP plans and schedules there is a critical need for following up with an extensive set of tracking mechanisms referred to as Shop Floor Control. The objective of Shop Floor Control is to track what actually happens with what was planned to happen.

If the system planned for producing 100 Widgets, and a planner released a work order for 100 Widgets, MRP assumes 100 Widgets will, in fact, be built in the time frame scheduled. If there was a quality problem and only 90 of the Widgets are useable, or if a machine broke down and the Widgets are going to be produced a week late, those are problems MRP needs to know about.

MRP breaks the production and purchasing plans down into a series of discrete production orders and purchase orders. It recommends the start date in anticipation of a completion date. Each of those orders must be closed out eventually, and progress along the way can be reported for work orders. Because reality is quite often much different from the theoretical plans, MRP is continually looking at the actual dates purchased parts arrive and production orders are completed, and looking at actual quantities received and produced. It is also tracking the actual orders received from customers, and replacing forecast dates and quantities with actuals.

With so much changing day to day, MRP must be constantly fed data from the receiving dock and the factory floor. Based on the feedback it gets from those places, planners and buyers receive a steady stream of necessary changes to the plan in order to get back to the Master Schedule. The more frequent and timely the feedback information, the more accurate MRP can be in its continual re-planning effort. This process of gathering actual results data – Shop Floor Control – is what turns MRP into a 'closed loop system'.

The basic principles driving MRP, and the basic MRP functions and logic we have described are common to the MRP function in all ERP systems, and they are largely unchanged since MRP was invented some fifty years ago. While the various providers of ERP software offer a wide range of features to make the system more user-friendly, and to make the data easier to evaluate, audit and manage, the heart and soul of all of them is identical.

MRP Detractors

MRP is subject to quite a bit of criticism lately, and for very good reason. It has some basic drawbacks that become more apparent as a manufacture embraces Lean Manufacturing.

For one, as has been discussed, it is usually forecast driven and forecasting is never accurate. As mentioned, if the forecast is 80% accurate (and that would actually be a much more accurate forecast than most manufactures experience) then 20% of the MRP system's recommendations are wrong, causing either under or over production.

The error in forecasting is compounded by data inaccuracy. As was also mentioned, inventory records must be highly accurate. Even relatively accurate inventory data is problematic, however, because inaccurate data compounds the problems with MRP – it does not average out. By this, we mean that if an 80% accurate forecast drives an MRP system along with 90% accurate inventory records, the result is 72% MRP effectiveness. The 80% accurate forecast is reduced by the fact that the information concerning the availability to meet that forecast with inventory is only 90% correct, so the calculation is $.8 \times .9 = .72$.

Maintaining near perfect inventory accuracy is not cheap in a company with quite a bit of inventory. Frequent cycle counting is necessary, along with a committed effort to identify and correct the root causes of inventory error. Even then it is a huge challenge since virtually all inventory errors are the result of human errors – people count things wrong, they misidentify items, items are put in the wrong bins, wrong boxes, or wrong locations; people transpose numbers or letters when entering inventory transactions into computers. A host of potential problems can arise, and humans will never perform error free.

MRP users attempt to minimize the impact of human error on inventory accuracy through the use of bar coding and scanners, and with the use of Radio Frequency Identification (RFID) tags. These approaches help, but they are expensive, and it still comes down to a human being putting the right bar code label on an item, or applying the right RFID tag.

MRP is by its very nature, transaction heavy. In order for the system to function it must be continually fed lots of information so it can accurately understand the situation in an ever-changing factory. The more timely management wants MRP information to be, the more frequently data must be captured and entered into the system. Of course supply chain people are not the only users of the system. Accounting relies on it as a cost collection vehicle, adding to the number of system transaction that must occur on the factory floor.

With dubious accuracy stemming from flawed forecast data, and erroneous inventory records it is rare to see a company using MRP to its full theoretical potential. Ignoring some of its' entire functionalities, such as capacity planning, is quite common. It is also common in MRP environments to see people working around the system with schedules on spreadsheets that are often downloaded MRP schedules modified to reflect realities that factory people know, but MRP doesn't.

The bottom line on MRP is that most users appreciate its ability to broadly plan volumes of components well into the future, and to plan future capacity requirements, but do not see it as an effective short term execution system. In the near term – today, tomorrow, next week – far too much accuracy is needed than MRP can effectively provide. Building the necessary accuracy into MRP would require an excessive amount of time and support labor, and shop floor personnel would spend way too much time entering data into the system.

MRP driven companies typically have an excessive amount of inventory simply because they have come to understand that having an excessive amount of inventory protects the plant from all of the problems that would arise from MRP's errors.

In subsequent chapters we will discuss supply chain management in some unique manufacturing environments. In some of these, MRP is an effective tool. In cases where the company builds few products every year, and those products are complicated with quite a few unique parts, and where standard lead times are quite long, MRP is a very effective tool.

This is for the simple reason that such companies are not forecast dependent and their inventory tends to be in small quantities purchased for a specific job. An example of such an MRP application would be the builder of large boats for private use, or ships for the Navy.

It is important to know what MRP can do well, and what its limitations are. More and more it's seen as a useful planning tool, but a limited execution tool. MRP's logic that 'explodes' Bills of Material and time phases requirements is very helpful for breaking a production plan down into its details. This can be very useful for your suppliers who need to understand their role in your production plans, and to identify capacity requirements in the future. As an execution tool, however, the transactions needed to support MRP and keep it up to date are often a drag on flow and provide little value relative to the time and expense of keeping the system up to date.

CHAPTER 14
Demand Pull – What It Is and How It Works

In discussing MRP systems we described it as a 'push' system, in which material and production were 'pushed' into inventory based on forecasts and master schedules of demand, planned ahead of customer orders. The alternative to push is a demand pull system. In 'pull' systems a minimum of inventory is set in place, and it is replaced as customer orders arrive and take from that inventory. In this manner, a customer order is shipped from the inventory, which triggers a signal to pull an equivalent amount through production to replace the items sold. The production pulls from a minimum inventory of purchased parts or raw materials, and a corresponding quantity is pulled from suppliers to replace the materials used. In this manner, a customer order has the effect of pulling inventory through the supply chain as if a string were tied from the finished item sold all the way back to the suppliers of the materials that went into the item.

The great benefit of such systems is that purchasing and production are always synchronized perfectly with actual demand. In push systems, to the degree that the forecast and master schedule are not identical to demand, there is always some purchasing and production of items that are not necessary. Push systems inevitably create an excess inventory. Of course push systems inevitably are wrong the other way, as well, in that they have a higher risk of failing to build what customers want.

The best example of a pull system is the one that, legend has it, inspired the Toyota Production Director Tai'ichi Ohno, to develop the kanban system, and that is the movement of milk cartons through a grocery store.

Typically a grocery store will have a quantity of milk in a refrigerated case accessible by the customers. There will also be a quantity of milk in crates in a large refrigerated room in the back of the store. Finally, the dairy company will make daily deliveries of milk to the store.

Throughout the day customers will 'pull' a gallon of milk from the case as they need it. At regular intervals a grocery store employee will bring enough milk from the crates in the back to replenish the milk customers have pulled. Each day when the dairy company makes its rounds, it will leave enough milk at the store to replace the milk cartons from the crates that were taken from the back room and put in the case. If on a given day, customers pull 75 gallons of milk from the case, 75 gallons will be taken from the back room to replenish that amount, and the next day the dairy company will leave 75 gallons of milk at the store.

If on the next day customers pull 125 gallons of milk, that amount will be pulled from the back room and through the dairy company. It is a simple system that is self-adjusting, assuring there is always enough milk to meet customer demand, without ever having too much milk.

What makes it work is having enough milk in the case to cover the maximum demand that might occur before the time when the employee who replenishes the case makes his rounds. If he refills the case every hour, the store must have an inventory in place in the case to cover peak customer demand for any hour.

Correspondingly, the store must keep enough inventory in place in the refrigerated room in the back to cover the maximum customer demand for a day – the interval between replenishments from the dairy company.

Toyota's kanban system operates on exactly the same principles. Finished goods inventory is the equivalent of the store's dairy case; and purchased inventory is the equivalent of the store's refrigerated back room. In between the two is production. Where the grocery store has an employee carry a few gallons of milk from the back room to the dairy case to replace the milk customers bought, Toyota has manufacturing produce the equivalent number of items customers bought.

The word 'kanban' actually means something along the lines of 'display card' in Japanese, and it denotes the cards used to send a signal to the preceding operation when something had been sold or used, to inform them when it was time to make or buy whatever was needed to replace the items.

Under a card-type kanban system like Toyota's, a card is attached to each finished item and when it is sold, the card is removed and sent to the operation that makes that item, which is their signal to make another one. That operation will pull from sub-assemblies or manufactured parts, each of them having their own kanban cards. Those cards are sent further upstream to wherever those sub-assemblies or components were made, telling them to make more.

There are countless approaches to kanban signals, and the method chosen is not important, so long as it works. Many companies use returnable containers where the box is the signal. Information is on the box indicating the part number and box quantity. When an operation uses all of the parts then the box is sent back to the operation that made the parts and it is their signal to make enough of the same part to refill the box.

In some highly automated environments the kanban signal is automated, as well. The robot assembling a product sends an electronic signal to the upstream operation telling it that the robot has just used some parts and more must be produced to replenish the ones used.

The nature of the pull signal is not important – the one for one (or at least lot size for lot size) replenishment philosophy is the important part.

Toyota's kanban, while a very effective method of demand pull, is not the only approach, nor was it the first. MIN-MAX systems are another form of demand pull, as are Two-Bin systems.

MIN-MAX is an approach to demand pull that, as the name implies, relies on a set minimum and maximum inventory level. When inventory falls to the point of reaching the minimum, it is replenished to the maximum. Say a part has a 500 maximum and a 300 minimum. When the on hand quantity drops to 300 minimum, enough parts are bought or made to get it back up to the 500 maximum. In this manner there is always enough inventory to cover peaks in demand (300), but there is a cap to prevent inventory from being over-bought or over-produced (500). While MIN-MAX tends to put more inventory into the plant than kanban, it really operates to the same principle of synchronizing purchasing and production to actual demand, rather than to a forecast or plan.

Two Bin systems are much like MIN-MAX. Under such an approach there might be two bins at a work station, each containing 250 parts. When one bin is empty, parts are ordered from other production areas or from suppliers to replace the 250. While waiting for those parts, production operates from the second bin. Eventually it is empty, at which point it is filled, but by then the first bin has been returned full. Again, there is a cap on the amount of inventory (whatever two bins can hold), a pre-set floor or minimum inventory to protect the plant from spikes or surges in demand, and the replenishment is based on actual usage rather than projected usage.

Another similar pull approach is Re-Order Point, which is simply a lot size driven version of MIN-MAX. Under a re-order point system, when inventory drops to a pre-determined level – the re-order point – another lot size of the part is either produced or purchased. For example, if the re-order point is 100 and the part is purchased in boxes or lot sizes of 50, when inventory reaches 100 another box is ordered, taking the inventory up to 150. The parts are then used as needed until the re-order point of 100 is reached again.

There is a widespread misconception that pull systems can only be applied to repetitive manufacturing environments, where large volumes of the same item are produced. That is simply not the case and, in fact, pull approaches can be applied in virtually every manufacturing environment with good results. Some are not very traditional, and some are not pure pull directly from customer demand, but they all synchronize adding to inventory either through purchasing or production by linking orders to the rate of actual demand, rather than planned or forecast demand.

Demand pull is not synonymous with Toyota-style kanban. Kanban is simply one effective means of deploying demand pull. Any approach that:

1. Drives production and purchasing directly from real customer demand, rather than a plan or a forecast
2. Has a cap on inventories preventing them from rising to a level not correlated directly to a one for one increase in actual demand
3. Sets a minimum or floor under which inventory will not drop that is based on assuring adequate coverage for spikes in customer demand over the replenishment lead time

…qualifies as demand pull, and provides the advantages of demand pull over forecast/master schedule driven push systems.

The diagram on the next page demonstrates one of the major advantages of demand pull over push production and inventory scheduling. A typical master schedule driven approach would commit the purchased steel to sub-assemblies and finished goods in anticipation of forecasted orders, and MRP generated orders would begin to drive the purchased steel into unique manufactured items well in advance of the receipt of customer orders. Under a demand pull approach, the steel inventory would not be committed to any one of the particular end items that use that particular steel until actual customer demand pulled it.

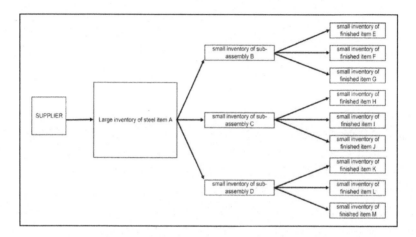

Another advantage of demand pull is that orders – both purchase orders and production orders – are self-created, and they create themselves immediately. Normally when a factory uses demand pull, rather than create multiple orders for the same item as MRP would do, a single blanket production order, and a large blanket purchase order are created, and all production or purchasing of the particular part goes against the blanket order. Converting the recognition of the need to make or buy something in an MRP environment into a production or purchase order often takes a few days. First, the demand must be picked up by a planner or buyer in the system. Then the order has to be created, which usually entails the creation of a packet of documentation to be issued to the shop floor, or sent to a supplier. With demand pull, no such delays are needed. The blanket order already exists, and all necessary documentation is already at the supplier or on the factory floor. All that is needed is the receipt of a pull signal – a kanban card, a returnable container, or some other simple notification, and things start to move. While it is usually a matter of days or even a week before MRP based approaches initiate a response to customer requirements, demand pull systems often respond within a few hours, or less.

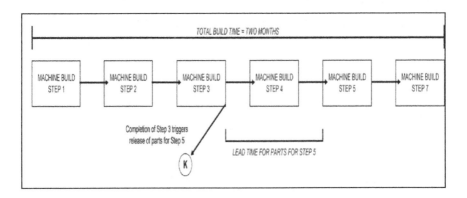

The previous graphic shows an example of pulling purchased parts, manufactured components or sub-assemblies based on progress in a long lead time build. The trigger to place an order for materials, while not based on replenishment as would be typical of demand pull, is based on confirmed demand for materials for a specific product at a specific time, based as closely as possible to reality, rather than plan.

In a typical MRP push environment, the parts needed for Step 5 on the router would be ordered based on a pre-set schedule – based on the plan date for performing step 5. If steps 1-4 were completed ahead of schedule the work would have to stop and wait for the parts for step 5. On the other hand, if steps 1-4 were completed behind schedule, the inventory of parts for step 5 would have to sit in stock until needed.

The next figure shows another variation on demand pull in a situation in which the manufacturing process is dominated by a severe capacity constraint. While the Theory of Constraints (TOC) will be addressed in detail in the next chapter, from a scheduling standpoint, the TOC "drum-buffer-rope" concept is a version of demand pull. In a capacity constrained process where the ability to produce determines whether customer orders can be met (as opposed to non-constrained processes where failure to deliver is driven by factory scheduling and long supplier lead time issues, rather than physical limitations of the ability to process materials), demand pull is driven by the bottleneck, as well as customer demand.

The drum-buffer-rope concept can basically be described as the rate of production through the bottleneck or constraint – OPERATION 5 in this example – sets the pace of production for the factory. There is no point in any other operation attempting to produce at a different pace since the constraint governs the overall output of the factory. The pace of the bottleneck is the drum, by which the entire plant operates.

The buffer idea is that a small quantity of work in process should always be sitting in queue in front of the constraint in order to assure that the constraint never runs out of work. Other operations can make up for time lost, but time lost at the constraint can never be recovered, so problems at Operations 1-4 should never be allowed to starve the constraint at Step 5 of work.

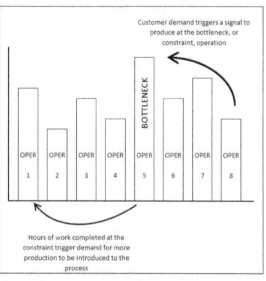

The rope is the actual demand pull application. As the graphic shows, production output at the constraint determines how much work should be introduced to the process at Operation 1. The amount of work introduced at Operation 1 is based on its load at the bottleneck. For instance, if the bottleneck at Operation 5 completes five hours of work, then five hours of Operation 5 work are begun at Operation 1. The priority at the Operation 5 bottleneck is the customer due date. Operations 6, 7 and 8 process the output of the Operation 5 bottleneck on a First In – First Out (FIFO) basis.

Again, while this is not a Toyota-style kanban, it is very much demand pull that has been adapted to the circumstances in which the factory operates.

The essential points to take from this chapter are that (1.) demand pull provides significant advantages over MRP-based push, especially in that it assures that purchases and production are synchronized with real customer demand, eliminating shortages and inventory excesses resulting from forecast and plan errors. Factory capacity is more dedicated to true demand and less wasted on production that will only sit in inventory. It also has the advantages of speed and simplicity. Rather than go through the cumbersome, costly and lengthy process of feeding information to an ERP system, and waiting for its output to create formal changes in the plan, demand pull mechanisms respond immediately to changes in demand or in production output.

(2.) Demand pull is not just kanban. It comes in a variety of forms and the manufacturer should apply demand pull processes that fit their environment. For most, a variation on Toyota kanban works best, but in circumstances in which kanban is not appropriate, the principles can and should be applied in a different manner.

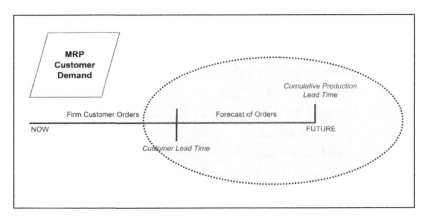

The graphic above is the same one shown in the previous chapter on how MRP/ERP works. The highlighted area – the gap between the factory's cumulative lead time and the customer lead times – is at the heart of the difference between push and pull approaches to inventory planning and factory scheduling. Push systems are based on forecasting and planning what will happen in that gap and then continually change the plans as reality becomes known.

Pull systems are based on putting a set quantity of inventory in place that have been calculated to cover variations in average demand that could occur during the gap, then having purchasing and production operate in a flexible manner, continually realigning itself with reality.

CHAPTER 15
The Theory of Constraints

The Theory of Constraints is a fundamental tool, a logical approach to understanding and managing flow, and it is an essential element of supply chain management. It was developed and explained by Eliyahu (Eli) Goldratt in his books, The Goal[ii], Theory of Constraints[iii] and others, and is taught through his Goldratt Institute (AGI) in Connecticut and around the world.

The basic idea is that every process has a bottleneck – a constraint – that limits the flow through the entire process. Optimizing flow through the constraint, and synchronizing flow through the rest of the process to the rate of flow through the constraint is critical to optimizing flow through the entire factory.

An easy way to understand the underlying concepts of the Theory of Constraints (TOC) is to consider the simple three step process of washing clothes. Step one is washing the clothes, step two is drying them, and step three is folding them and putting them away.

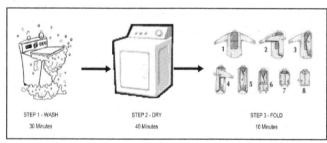

STEP 1 - WASH
30 Minutes

STEP 2 - DRY
40 Minutes

STEP 3 - FOLD
10 Minutes

Let's assume it takes thirty minutes to wash the clothes, forty minutes to dry them, and ten minutes to fold them, for a total process cycle time of eighty minutes as indicated in the figure above. As the next figure indicates, the first load would be finished in eighty minutes, and the second load would be complete in 120 minutes. Note that the second load would have to sit after washing is complete for ten minutes while it waits for the dryer to complete its cycle on the first load.

MINUTES

	LOAD 1	LOAD 2
130		
120		FOLD
110		
100		DRY
90		
80	FOLD	
70		WAIT
60	DRY	
50		WASH
40		
30		
20	WASH	
10		

If we were to invest in a new washing machine that can reduce the time from thirty minutes to twenty minutes, the logical assumption would be that we can reduce the time to complete a load of laundry from eighty minutes to seventy minutes. This is true, *but only once.*

As you can see in the figure on the right, the first load took only seventy minutes, but the time required to do two loads did not go down by twenty minutes – only ten minutes from 120 down to 110. What happened was that the time spent waiting for the dryer increased by ten minutes for the second load.

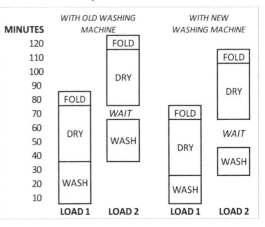

In fact, if we look at the time required to do six loads, the effect is even more dramatic, as the next figure indicates:

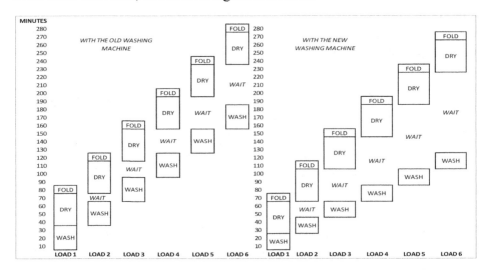

Rather than save ten minutes per load, all that has been accomplished has been to create a greater level of inventory in front of the dryer. This is because the washing machine is not the constraint in the process. The constraint is the dryer. At forty minutes per load, it is the slowest operation in the process and it will determine how much laundry is completed over the course of the day.

Since the dryer is the constraint, however, finding a dryer that can work ten minutes faster is an improvement for the overall process. As the next figure indicates, with a faster dryer the time required to complete six loads is reduced from 280 minutes to 220 minutes – sixty minutes, or ten minutes per load, faster. Improving the rate of throughput at the constraint resulted in an improvement for the entire process.

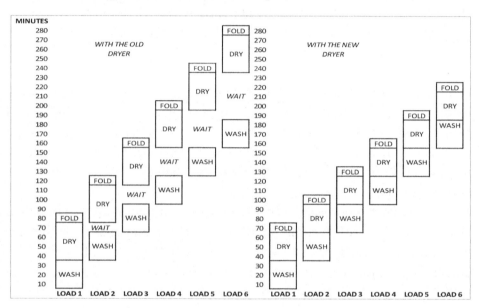

This demonstrates the fundamental economic principle behind the TOC – that, as Goldratt puts it, '*an improvement at the constraint is an improvement for the system, while an improvement anywhere else is a mirage.*' In terms of the amount of product going out the door and sold to customers, speeding the rate of output from an operation other than the constraint actually accomplishes nothing. At the end of the day, the plant will

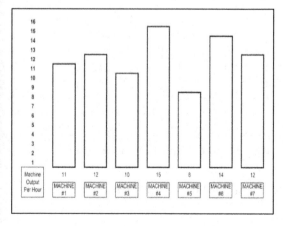

ship, and customers will pay for, the output of the constraint. While improving the speed of the dryer creates the appearance of greater efficiency, it actually only accomplishes building inventory in front of the constraint.

The inverse of that principle is also true. That is that time lost at the constraint can never be recovered, while time lost anywhere else can be. Put another way, an hour lost at the constraint is an hour lost for the system, while an hour lost anywhere else may not really have been lost at all. For this reason, it is essential that the performance of the bottleneck, or constraint operation, be managed carefully, and that no time is lost.

Goldratt would correctly point to the flow in the previous figure as an anomaly since capacity – or the throughput rate for both the washer and dryer are perfectly balanced. He would suggest that, due to a changing mix of products, improvements in the performance of machines and people, and other factors that capacity is never balanced for an entire process – or if it is, it will not stay balanced for long. He urges balancing the level of flow rather than wasting time and money in a fruitless attempt to balance capacity.

The TOC approach to balancing flow is through a concept called "Drum-Buffer-Rope". Getting out of the laundry realm and into a factory, the best way to understand Drum, Buffer and Rope is with the simple diagram at the bottom of the previous page. There are seven manufacturing steps in this process with varying output capabilities ranging from eight to fifteen parts per hour.

The operation with the lowest output is Machine #5, which can only produce eight parts per hour. It is the constraint that limits the output for the entire process, and

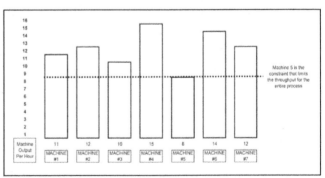

any operation producing at a rate greater than that will simply build inventory without adding anything to sales revenue. Therefore, what is needed is a mechanism to assure that (1.) the constraint is able to achieve its rate of eight per hour, and (2.) the rest of the process does not exceed the rate of eight per hour.

The next figure demonstrates the application of the Drum-Buffer-Rope concept to the process.

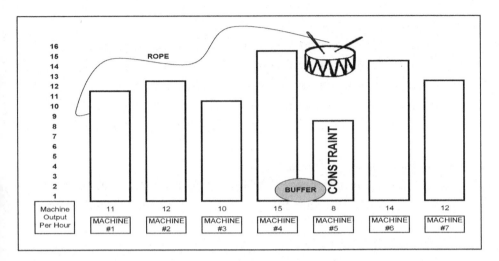

The 'Drum' is the rate of production – in this case, eight per hour. The rate of production at the constraint sets the pace – the drumbeat – for the rest of the process.

The 'Buffer' is a quantity of inventory always kept in front of the constraint to be sure it never runs out of work. As was mentioned previously, a loss of production at the constraint can never be recovered, so it is essential to never starve the constraint. The purpose of the buffer is to assure that if a mistake or a problem occurs upstream, in Operations 1-4, those problems do not affect the constraint.

Finally, the 'Rope' is a signal – a demand pull signal, in fact – linking the rate of production at the constraint to the beginning of the process. In some applications the rope is tied all the way back to the supplier. The purpose of the "Rope', or signal, is to be sure that inventory is introduced to the process at the same rate the constraint produces.

There are also a few other important principles involved in the TOC that deserve mention. First, it is important to keep in mind that there is always a constraint in every process. In the figure above if we were to find a way to double the throughput of Machine #5 so that it could produce 16 units per hour, it would no longer be the constraint. However,

Machine #3 would emerge as the new constraint since its throughput capability of ten per hour would now be the limiting factor for this process. Just as Machine #5 was treated as a constraint, now Machine #3 would be. Its output would serve as the drum, the buffer would be moved to protect it, and the rope would be tied from Machine #3 to the beginning of the process.

Second, it is important to realize that the constraint in a process may very well be a non-manufacturing step. It can, and often is, a support or business step. For instance, in custom machining or manufacturing environments it is not uncommon to find that the work of preparing a customer order for production – creating drawings and specifications, machine programs and so forth – is the constraint. There is ample machine and personnel capacity, but the challenge is to optimize the paperwork flow to get the information from customers to production. In some cases the constraint is in the order entry step, or the customer credit approval step.

Finally, it is not uncommon to find the constraint is outside the plant entirely, at a supplier operation. The gating issue may be a supplier's inability to provide the plant with a steady flow of acceptable parts and materials.

The rationalization for over-producing at the non-bottleneck operations is most often labor efficiency, coupled with set-up times. In order to minimize labor costs in the face of lengthy machine set-up times, production wants to over produce at a non-constraint operation in order to make the most of the operator's time while the machine is set up. This will be discussed in greater detail in the chapters dealing with lean manufacturing, but it is important to know that, while such practices may occasionally be necessary, there are substantial costs and negative quality implications that offset whatever labor cost benefits may be possible from over-production. At the very least, it is important that any over-production take place with management's eyes 'wide open' to the fact that over-production is occurring and to what extent.

The important points to take away from this chapter, in addition to a basic understanding of the Theory of Constraints, are (1.) in order to optimize flow it is essential that the people executing the supply chain scheme always know where the constraints are in every process, and that the scheduling methods take them into account. The extent to which it is important to formalize the application of the TOC in any individual plant depends on a number of factors, including how unbalanced plant capacity is, and how much overall capacity is available. The more capacity constrained the plant is the more important it is to have a very keen focus on constraint resources.

CHAPTER 16
Variability of Demand

One of the critical inputs to determining the amount of inventory necessary to reliably meet customer demand is the rate of variation in the demand. The chart to the right demonstrates fairly low variation in demand rate. It is consistent and predictable; and it is easy to forecast. Little inventory above the weekly average of fifty units is necessary to assure the next customer order can be filled in a timely manner.

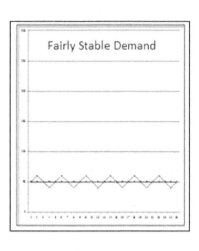

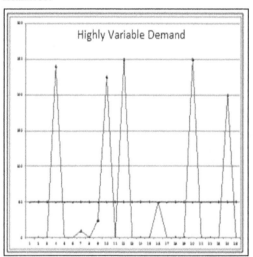

On the other hand, the chart on the left indicates a widely variable rate of demand, with numerous weeks in which there is no demand, interrupted by weeks with extremely high demand. Quite obviously a much greater inventory level is needed to meet customer demand when it fluctuates so greatly, even though the demand level for the item on the right is the same fifty per week average.

Many companies make the mistake of using the historical average demand rate as the basis for setting inventory levels. While average demand is a useful figure in assessing the long term demand for a given item, it is wholly inadequate for determining how much inventory is needed at any specific point in time to meet the customer orders that might be placed that week.

If an inventory policy of four weeks average demand (4 X the 50 per week average for both items) were in place for these two items, having 200 units in stock would be far more inventory than needed to protect the item in the figure above; and not enough to meet half of the orders placed for the item in the figure to the left.

The correct statistical calculation to use in gauging the rate of variation in demand for purposes of inventory calculation is standard deviation, represented by the Greek symbol σ, or 'sigma'. The logic is exactly the same as that which forms the basis for Motorola's Six Sigma®[iv] approach. The crux of Six Sigma is that processes must be robust enough to handle a wide range of possible events.

An analogy often used to explain Six Sigma is the width of a car relative to the width of the garage door. If the car is six feet wide, theoretically a garage door six feet one inch wide is acceptable. As everyone knows, however, the likelihood of consistently moving the car in and out of that garage without problems is very low. A wider garage door increases the probability of entering and exiting the garage without problems. How much wider the garage door must be than the car depends on the amount of deviation from the centerline we can reasonably expect to occur.

In terms of inventory, putting inventory in place that meets forecast demand exactly is the equivalent of a garage door precisely the width of the car. There is no room for error – or deviation from the theoretically perfect outcome. If the forecast is off, or if the customer orders even a small quantity over the historical average, a shipment will be missed.

Standard deviation is a measure of the degree of variation, or dispersion, of data from a midpoint. It is calculated as the square root of the average of the squared differences of each value in a data series from the mean (or average). The math is readily available as an Excel formula, as well as in most scientific calculators.

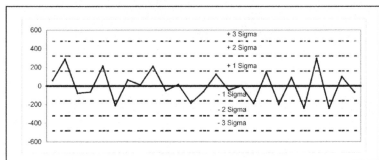

In the previous chart a series of data is displayed bouncing around a mean of zero. The dotted lines indicate standard deviations (Sigma).

The chart on the right correlates probabilities with standard deviation

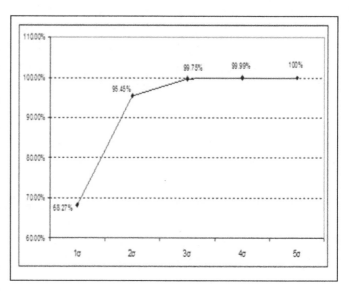

values. In the chart on the previous page note the dotted lines above and below the zero average line marked "+1 Sigma" and "-1 Sigma". Those lines indicate one standard deviation above and below the mean of zero. Referring now to the chart on the top of this page you can see that one standard deviation correlates to 68.27%. This means that the statistical probability of the next point on the graph on the previous page falling between the +/- 1 Sigma lines is 68.27%.

Following the same logic, the probability of the next point falling between the +/- 2 Sigma lines is 95.45%; and the probability of the next point falling between the +/- 3 standard deviation lines is 99.75%.

According to Six Sigma logic, whenever a process is set at 3 standard deviations above and 3 standard deviations below the mean, it is a process capable of performing correctly at close enough to statistical certainty. (Hence "Six Sigma" – 3 sigma over, 3 sigma under the mean).

The calculations for safety stocks and kanban quantities in a demand pull environment are the same. The table to the right demonstrates a demand pattern for two items – Item A and Item B – for a historical 26 week period. At the bottom are the results of some basic mathematical calculations. Notice that both items had a total demand of 1,300 units over the 26 weeks, and as a result both items average 50 per week.

It is also important to note that the 2σ and 3σ calculation is simply one standard deviation times two and three respectively.

As the chart below indicates, the demand for Item A is relatively flat and consistent. An inventory of 74 units - the average plus 2 standard deviations - is adequate to assure on time delivery.

	Weekly Demand	
	Item A	Item B
	58	212
	63	0
	28	0
	71	21
	44	0
	61	138
	55	0
	45	0
	37	0
	29	0
	54	124
	51	0
	37	0
	63	0
	51	178
	69	230
	65	0
	42	0
	38	0
	55	0
	60	207
	48	0
	54	0
	36	0
	47	190
	39	0
Total	1,300	1,300
Average	50	50
1σ	12.0	84.5
2σ	24.0	168.9
3σ	36.0	253.4

If we were to use a simple average and put in place an inventory of three weeks average demand, or 150 units, we would end up with twice as much inventory with no improvement in our ability to deliver on time.

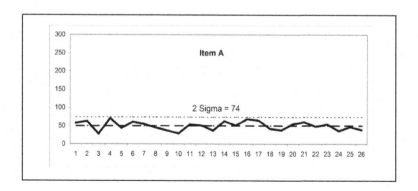

On the other hand, the chart below demonstrates a highly variable demand pattern for Item B. Although this item has the same fifty per week average, the amount of inventory required to assure availability for customer delivery is radically different. For this item, two standard deviations plus the average calls for an inventory of 169 units. In this case, carrying a simple average of three weeks of the average historical demand would result in missing customer delivery requirements in five of the 26 weeks (weeks 1, 15, 16, 21 and 25), for an availability rate of only 81%. The important points to take from this discussion are that (1.) the amount of inventory needed to assure on time delivery to customers is highly dependent on the variability of the demand pattern, and (2.) the more sporadic the demand is, the more inventory will be needed.

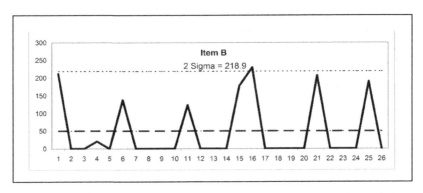

In subsequent chapters we will describe how variability, along with lead times and lot sizes, are used in a very specific manner to determine necessary inventory levels to meet specific lead time requirements and specific on time delivery objectives. Achieving those objectives without as much inventory can only be accomplished by reducing the impact of those critical input variables. It is impossible to meet short lead time delivery goals with minimal inventory in the face of highly sporadic demand rates.

It is a fallacy to believe that inventories can be reduced simply by expecting supply chain personnel to work more diligently if the inventories have been established by sound methods, properly taking into account rates of variability, lead times and lot sizes. If established properly, reducing the inventory levels without smoothing demand patterns, shortening lead times or reducing lot sizes will inevitably result in a deterioration of on time delivery performance.

The most common cause of sporadic demand is a misperception that higher volumes are more economical for the manufacturer. In many cases, customers are encouraged to order sporadically – ordering large, infrequent quantities rather than a steady stream off small orders – by offering them volume discounts. While there may be cases in which such economies exist, management should be aware of the disruption in factory flow and the corresponding large inventories that such order patterns cause.

CHAPTER 17
Lead Times

The second major driver of inventory levels is lead time. In order to properly understand lead time the first step is to clarify the terminology. The basic elements that determine the level of inventory required in the supply chain are supplier lead time, manufacturing lead time and customer lead time. Obviously, in the series of enterprises linked together in the supply chain, one entity's customer lead time is the next entity's supplier lead time. All of our discussion, unless otherwise indicated are in terms of the lead time as they relate to *you* – assuming *you* are a manufacturer within the supply chain with upstream suppliers and downstream customers.

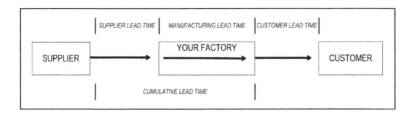

As the graphic above indicates, there is another lead time term – 'cumulative lead time', which is the total of your supplier and manufacturing lead times.

Supplier Lead Time

Your supplier lead time is the total time required from the time you know you will need parts or materials from a supplier until the parts or materials arrive. This lead time typically is the sum of the following basic elements-

Internal communications time

This can range from a matter of minutes to several days but there is a time delay from the time you establish a requirement for production that will require supplier provided materials until your procurement personnel are aware of the requirement.

Order processing time

This too can range from minutes to days, but there is some time required for procurement personnel to perform any quoting and processing of purchase order documentation that may be required.

Supplier processing time

The supplier may ship the material from inventory, in which case their processing time will be fairly short, or the supplier may manufacture to order which drives much longer processing times

Transit time

This is the time required for the materials to be physically shipped from the supplier's location to yours.

It is important to take into account the elements of supplier lead time that are actually within your scope of operations (internal communications and order processing) when calculating and assessing inventory requirements. While the bulk of the lead time is usually the supplier's time, the time consumed by your internal processes cannot be ignored when determining necessary inventories.

Manufacturing Lead Time

Manufacturing lead time is the total time required for material to flow from your receiving function to shipment. It is important to subtract work in process inventories from the total and treat them separately.

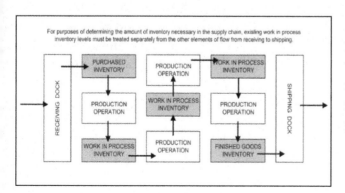

Generally, the manufacturing lead time is the total time required for the next item purchased to flow from the time it

101

is withdrawn from purchased inventory to the time it is put into finished goods or shipped if there is not a finished goods inventory. (See the flow chart the previous page). This is usually somewhat longer than the theoretical time it would take for an item to flow directly from one operation to the next throughout the factory. It includes such things as waiting time due to capacity imbalances, quality inspection time, time for parts to be moved from one area of the factory to another, and so forth.

The chart below indicates the range of causes for inventory to exist within the manufacturing process in addition to the time required to actually process the material. Inventory that exists as a result of these manufacturing problems should be considered as part of the manufacturing lead time.

Another common driver of work in process inventory is the scheduling cycle. Although it is usually an inefficient method of scheduling production it is simpler to plan production in standard time buckets – usually weeks. For example, all customer orders received this week would be machined next week, finished or chemically treated the following week, then assembled, packed and shipped the next week. This creates work in process inventory as the production completed in one week sits waiting to be further processed next week. This work in process inventory should also be included in the manufacturing lead time.

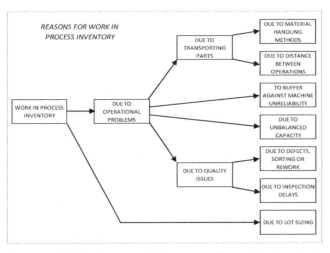

A third standard cause of work in process inventory is outside work. For example, parts may be sent outside of the factory to a third party or another location for cleaning, anodizing, painting, etc... The time required for these activities is part of the manufacturing lead time.

The inventories normally excluded from the manufacturing lead time calculation are those set deliberately by policy, usually for strategic reasons or for risk mitigation. In some circumstances management may decide that, regardless of normal supply chain operational considerations a 'safety stock' of some pre-determined amount must be kept at some point in the process. Examples of this might be where there is a sole source of supply and management wants to insure against a catastrophic event at the supplier plant; or the terms of a customer contract mandate that some amount of inventory must be kept at some stage of production; or management wants to have the ability to quickly respond to an unlikely but potentially lucrative sales opportunity. These inventories are not part of the manufacturing lead time calculation.

The reader will note that 'inventory' and 'lead time' are used as nearly interchangeable terms. The relationship between time and inventory is simple but critical to clearly understand because it is at the heart of supply chain strategy, design, and execution.

As the chart on the right illustrates, if there is a work in process inventory, or merely a box or skid of 50 of some item, and that item is 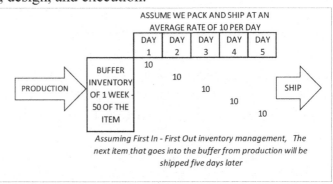 shipped at a rate of ten per day, it will take five days before those items are shipped. If there were 60 in the inventory it would be six days before the last one in is shipped. There is a direct, linear correlation between inventory levels and manufacturing lead time. The more inventory there is in the plant, the longer it will be before the next item to arrive in receiving leaves the plant via shipping (on average).

The most simple and most accurate way to determine your total manufacturing lead time is to count the number of an item at any and every stage of the manufacturing process, and divide the total by the average number of that item shipped per day. If you have 900 widgets, for example, in process between purchased inventory and finished goods (or shipping if there are no finished goods), and you ship products with 45 widgets embedded in them per day, then the lead time is 20 days (900 widgets in process ÷ 45 widgets shipped per day).

The manufacturing lead time for a product is equal to the longest manufacturing lead time for any of its significant components. This is a very important point. Assume a product has the following bill of material with these associated lead times calculated by the above method:

Component	Quantity Per	Lead Time	Cost
Widgets	1	20 days	$ 6
Brackets	4	14 days	$ 2
Base	1	26 days	$ 8
Wires	2	12 days	$ 1
Motor	1	18 days	$16

The manufacturing lead time for this product is 26 days – the lead time for the Base – because it has the longest lead time of all of the components needed to make the product. That is an important point to realize even though the average lead time is 16 days. This is because the time required for a completed product to flow through the factory is that of the component or sub-assembly with the longest lead time. In other words, while brackets and wires may be able to get to the final operation very quickly they will not go anywhere until they are mated with a base, which takes the longest time.

It is also important to understand the difference between lead time and 'Inventory Turnover', or 'Inventory Turns'. Inventory turnover is a financial measure of the rate at which dollars of inventory are flowing. As a result, it would put twice as much weight on the lead time, or flow rate, of motors as it would on bases because motors tie up twice as many dollars. If the factory keeps a very low inventory of expensive materials,

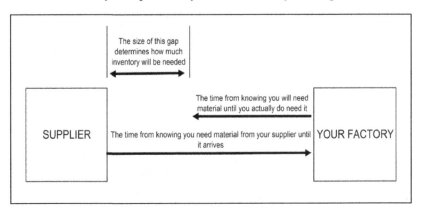

but an excess of inventory of lower cost items due to production problems as described previously, it is quite possible for the plant to have good financial inventory turns, while providing poor delivery lead time capabilities to customers.

The amount of inventory that must be placed in the supply chain is actually not a function of lead times, but of lead time gaps. As the chart on the previous page indicates, it is the difference between when you actually need the part or component and the length of time it will take to get it that matters, not just the absolute time required to get the part.

In many operations your knowledge that you will need a part comes with little advanced warning. A customer order comes and you must produce quickly to fill the order. If you are a capital equipment manufacturer, however, there are apt to be parts you know you will need, but you will not need them for some time until you reach the stage of production at which they will be applied to the product.

If, for instance, you need the part in one week, but your supplier lead time is three weeks, it is the gap of two weeks between your requirement and their lead time that must be protected by inventory – not the entire three week supplier lead time.

The same is true of your customer lead times, as shown in this graphic:

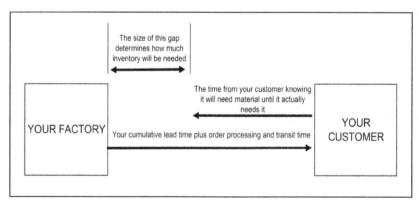

It is the gap between the length of time it takes you to produce and the time at which a customer requires the product that creates the need for inventory, rather than your absolute manufacturing lead time. If your customer is a retailer, they most likely do not know that they need one of your products until a consumer buys one from their store shelf, and then they need for one to replenish the shelf is almost immediate. On the other hand, if your customer makes complicated, custom machinery, they may not need your product for several weeks after they have begun working on a machine for a customer order.

Note that lead time is just one of the critical inputs to determining inventory levels – along with variability and lot sizes – but it is a critical input. As a result it is very important to know what your lead times are. Equally important is the understanding that regardless of how much lead times contribute to the inventory calculation relative to the impact of the other input variables, the inventory in your supply chain will always have a direct correlation to lead times, and all efforts to reduce supplier and manufacturing lead times can directly generate inventory reductions.

CHAPTER 18
Lot Sizes

While theoretically optimum inventory levels are determined solely by variability and lead time, actual inventory levels are also impacted by lot size concerns. For example, if a statistical analysis determines that, based on historical variability patterns and the lead time gaps an inventory of 112 parts should be kept in stock, but the parts are purchased in lot sizes of 25, the manufacturer must either carry an inventory of 100 parts, or 125.

It is for this reason that lot sizes >1 always have a negative effect on inventory levels, availability rates or both. Carrying less than the theoretically optimum level of inventory is rarely a good idea. As the chart from Chapter 14 indicates, the relationship between inventory levels and service levels is not linear. Carrying

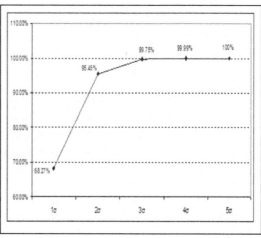

10% less inventory than that which statistically assures a given availability rate quite often results in an availability rate more than 10% less than what is actually needed.

In the example above, the ideal inventory was 112 parts and the lot size was 25, so the inventory should be 125, or about 12% more inventory than needed. If the lot size is 50, however, then the necessary inventory to meet availability requirements would be 150, or 34% more inventory than needed. The alternative, again, is to accept less than necessary availability rates by only carrying 100 of the 112 parts needed.

It is because of this statistical reality that any time lot sizes are greater than one, excess inventory or degraded availability rates are inevitable. They cause inventories to be 'rounded up' which creates excess, or 'rounded down' creating shortfalls.

The primary drivers of purchasing and customer lot sizes are freight considerations and volume discount pricing. Manufacturing lot sizes are typically driven by the time needed to set up machines or to change a production line from one product to another.

While various strategies and techniques exist to reduce lot sizes without losing some of the economic benefits in freight cost and bulk purchasing and will be discussed in later chapters, it is important for supply chain architects and managers to look at and monitor lot sizes very closely. Far too often they are established without a sound basis, or are not updated and reduced as circumstances change.

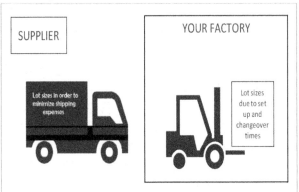

For many years, lot sizes were the subject of considerable attention as various approaches to Economic Order Quantity (EOQ) theory were advanced. However, EOQ has fallen out of favor as a valid approach to supply chain management with the expansion of Lean Manufacturing.

EOQ is a mathematical theory that relies heavily on assumptions of fixed cost allocations, assumptions concerning inventory carrying costs and calculated costs to create orders relative to machine set up times. It has been debunked by Lean practitioners largely based on the notion that the time required to set up machines is waste, as are most inventory carrying costs and order generating costs. Lean theory takes the stance that EOQ just attempts to find an optimal balance between different forms of waste, and rather than analyzing waste, it should simply be eliminated altogether. If set up times can be reduced to insignificance, and top down schedules with associated order costs can be replaced by self-managing kanbans and pull systems, there is no reason for lot sizes to be greater than one. In practical terms, that means lot sizes should be equal to real demand, even if that demand is very low.

MRP systems are highly dependent on lot sizes, and while the concept of EOQ actually dates back almost 100 years[v], the modern versions of it are largely products of the 1980's and '90's, the heyday of

MRP. MRP systems, in theory, assure that there is one half lot size of everything in inventory at all times. This logic, coupled with typically long set-up times which in turn creates large lot sizes, is the reason why factories driven by MRP have substantially more work in process inventory than those driven by demand pull approaches.

Regardless, the important lessons to take from this chapter are that (1.) purchasing and production lot sizes have a direct bearing on necessary inventory levels; (2.) the effect of lot sizes on inventory is always negative and often significantly negative; and (3.) supply chain management should be diligent in assuring lot sizes are always as small as possible.

SECTION III
Deployment and Execution Approaches

Armed with direction concerning the company's strategic requirements, and an understanding of the basic principles and techniques, the next logical step is to determine precisely how the supply chain will be structured, how materials will flow from suppliers and through the company's operations, and out to customers.

How this will be done depends largely on the type of business – distributor, manufacturer, or both – and if a manufacturer, does the company make products to stock or make them to order.

The first step will be to make decisions concerning inventory – where in the supply chain inventory must be kept, and how much to keep on hand. Next we will discuss the best practices for scheduling and controlling manufacturing operations as well as controlling the flow of material through the plant. Finally we will discuss supplier interface issues and techniques, as well as freight and logistics.

There is rarely a 'one size fits all' supply chain solution for any business. Most have a combination of stock and non-stock products and components, a wide range of supplier types, locations and capabilities, and an equally wide range of customers, each with unique requirements. It is quite common to see a business deploying a combination of forecast driven, MRP type push thinking and Lean demand pull principles mixed with a liberal dose of the Theory of Constraints.

While each of those approaches has its advocates, they all have strengths and weaknesses, and it is a mistake to believe that any one approach is inherently or universally superior to the others. The challenge to the supply chain professional's creativity and wisdom is in devising a combination of different techniques that most perfectly fits the business' unique situation. This next section is intended to help with that task.

CHAPTER 19
Inventory Planning for Make to Stock

Determining the right amount of inventory to carry is perhaps the most important supply chain execution decisions a company will make. The logic is the same whether the company is a manufacturer, a distributor, or both. Within each of those industry types there may be unique factory scheduling and purchasing processes, but both those processes have the same objective which is assuring the proper inventory levels.

Planning inventory is primarily a statistical endeavor. The information in the previous three chapters: Variability of demand, Lead times, and Lot sizes are the primary inputs. There are other factors to consider, as well, such as non-statistical management decisions, but these are the basic factors to consider.

Setting the inventory level depends on the answers to these four questions:

1. If I use or sell some of the inventory, how long will it take to replenish it?
2. What is the demand for the item likely to be during the time I am waiting for the replenishment to arrive?
3. How many do I have to buy (or make) at a time?
4. What is my availability objective?

The availability objective

Taking the last question first, it is important to recognize that it is statistically impossible, and quite often practically impossible, to assure 100% availability of everything the company needs. There are simply too many potential unknowns to have enough inventory to protect against every conceivable event that could disrupt the flow or cause an unexpected spike in customer demand. As you will see when the math is explained, the amount of inventory necessary to assure a 99.9% availability level is radically higher in most cases, than the amount of inventory needed to assure a 98% availability level. As you move closer to attempting to assure 100%, the amount of inventory needed increases at a very dramatic rate.

In any event, most firms set an objective of 98% as the optimum inventory planning goal, with perhaps a few selected items (by management decision) at something closer to 100% in order to assure near perfect service levels for specific items or for specific customers.

The Formula

The starting mathematical formula for determining the right inventory levels, assuming a weekly replenishment cycle and a 98% availability goal, is as follows:

$$\left(\begin{array}{c} \text{Average} \\ \text{weekly} \\ \text{demand} \end{array} \ \text{X} \ \begin{array}{c} \text{Order} \\ \text{Frequency} \\ \text{(in weeks)} \end{array} \right) + \left(2.2\sigma \ \text{X} \ \left(\left(\begin{array}{c} \text{Repenishment} \\ \text{Lead Time} \end{array} - \begin{array}{c} \text{Customer} \\ \text{Lead Time} \end{array} \right) \div 2^* \right) \right)$$

*result of Replen LT - Customer LT
÷ 2 cannot be less than 1

Average Weekly Demand

Average weekly demand is simply that – the historical average weekly customer demand for the item. In most cases, looking at the most recent 26 weeks is sufficient to obtain a satisfactory sample size. There are exceptions to this 'last 26 weeks' approach, however. The most common reason for using a different historical period is in cases where there is a significant seasonal demand for the item. In that case, using the most recent 26 week period that correlates with the upcoming 26 weeks is the best approach. Put another way, rather than using the last six months data, use the six months before that so you are looking at data that more closely correlates with the season you are entering.

(Note: Do not worry about the fact that the forecast for the upcoming future may be higher or lower than the past. We will discuss adjusting for that later.)

Order Frequency (in weeks)

The order frequency is simply how often the item is re-ordered from the supplier, or scheduled for production in the factory. If you place an order for the item with the supplier every week, then the order frequency is 1. If you look at your requirements once a month, then the order frequency is 4 – because you order it about every four weeks.

The more often you order an item, the more steady the flow of that item into inventory is, and the less inventory you have to carry.

2.2σ

This is the mathematical representation of 2.2 standard deviations, as was discussed in Chapter 14. There is a direct correlation between the standard deviation figure and the probability of the order pattern falling between the bounds of the standard deviation figure above and below the average. If the average is 50 per week, for instance, and the 2.2σ figure is 12, then there is a 98% probability of next week's orders falling between 38 and 62, based on the historical rate of fluctuation in weekly demand.

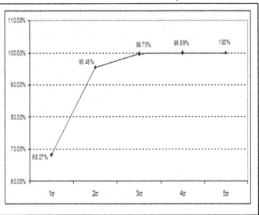

As the chart from Chapter 14 indicates, the number of standard deviations correlates with the probability of having the necessary inventory. If you use the same formula, but with 1σ instead of 2.2σ, the resulting formula will call for less inventory, but your probability of having the necessary amount of inventory to meet customer demand drops from 98% to 68%. Note the diminishing returns toward the top of the chart. Increases in inventory that would result from using a higher standard deviation figure result in less and less improvements in availability.

Also note that there are a number of ways to calculate standard deviation (although they all attempt to get at the same thing). It is recommended that the basic 'Sample Standard Deviation' formula be used. It is the simplest and easiest to find. Note as well, 'standard deviation' is one of the basic functions available in Excel and most other spreadsheets and is very easy to find and use. Given the margin of error in some of the other inputs to the formula there is little to be gained by spending much time or effort in attempting to refine the standard deviation math.

Replenishment Lead Time

This is the total lead time from the time an order is placed with the supplier or a schedule is released to production until the items are available in inventory. For the most part this is fairly straightforward. The only cautionary note is that, in manufacturing environments in which no raw material or purchased inventory is carried, the replenishment lead time includes both the time required to procure the necessary materials *plus* the time required in production (the Cumulative Lead Time).

Customer Lead Time

This is also straightforward. It reflects the shipment policy of the company. If the policy is to ship the same day an order is received – or within a few days – and the replenishment lead time exceeds the customer lead time (for example, the company strives to ship within 24 hours of receipt of an order and the replenishment lead time is two weeks), then the customer lead time for purposes of inventory planning is zero.

It is only in cases in which the customer lead time exceeds one week *and* the customer lead time is less than the replenishment lead time that a figure other than zero should be used.

Multiplying by 2

The last element of the formula is to divide the lead time gap – Replenishment Lead Time minus Customer Lead Time – in half. This is based on a general assumption that upward spikes in demand (weeks in which demand exceed the average) will only occur in half of the weeks, while the other half will experience downward order weeks). It is logical to ask, if this is the case, won't the left over inventory from the low demand weeks be available to cover the higher demand in the other weeks? The answer is no, it will not. Because a smaller replenishment order will be placed following a low demand week, that inventory will never be in place to cover the spikes in demand.

This is Demand Pull Inventory – Not Safety Stock

It is very important to recognize that this is the calculation for the inventory targets to be used in a demand pull application. The application of it is to simply place replenishment orders at the replenishment intervals to replace that which has been sold or used from inventory. It is not a safety stock inventory to be set in place, with orders for forecast demand placed in addition to this inventory.

In a kanban environment, the use of items from the inventory calculated in this manner would trigger the release of a kanban card either to purchasing or production which would constitute the notice that a production order or a purchase order should be generated to replace the items used. (Note that in a kanban environment, this is often not true. Blanket production and purchase orders are often established and the kanban card triggers a release against the existing blanket order.)

In an MRP/ERP environment, the planned demand function is essentially turned off and the resulting inventory requirement from this calculation is entered into the safety stock field, which automatically generates a replenishment need every week or every day as the system seeks to get back to the safety stock level. Again, the fact that the safety stock field is used in an MRP/ERP system does not mean that this inventory should be treated as safety stock. It is essential that the planned demand for the items be shut off or the system will drive far more inventory than necessary into the system.

Lot Sizes

Lot sizes are not actually an element of the target inventory calculation, but they can have a significant impact on the resulting actual inventory.

If the lot sizes are 1, for instance, meaning you can order any quantity you want from the supplier or the factory to replenish the inventory, you will rarely actually have the target inventory on hand. For example, let's assume the target inventory is 150 and the average demand is 25 per week, and the customer lead time is zero (you ship upon receipt of order) and the supplier lead time is one week. At the end of this week you compare the target inventory of 150 with the actual on hand – let's say the actual on hand is 120 because you shipped 30. You would place an order with the supplier for 30 to replace the items shipped. Those items are received in a week, but this would not take you back up to the 150 target because by then you sold 25 more leaving only 125 on hand after the 30 are received, so you place another order for the 25 that you are below target. Of course by the time those come in you have sold more again, so you are constantly chasing but never reaching the target inventory level.

How much inventory will you actually have? If the lot sizes are one then the theoretical actual will be the target minus one half of the weekly demand. Of course it will vary from week to week, but over time the inventory on any given day in the example cited will be the 150 minus half of the 25 per week average, or 137.5 units – about 92% of the target. Lower variation in demand will improve this figure proportionately.

On the other hand, let's look at the results should the item need to be purchased in lot sizes of 50. Now if we assume the same situation - the target inventory is 150 and the average demand is 25 per week, and the customer lead time is zero (you ship upon receipt of order) and the supplier lead time is one week – when you get to the end of the week and the actual on hand inventory is 120 you cannot order only the 30 needed to get back to the target – you must order 50. The 50 arrive in a week, and you have sold another 25 by then, so the resulting inventory is 145. Again although you now only need 5 to reach the target but, again, you have to order 50. A week later the 50 have arrived and you sold another 25 but, due to lot sizing, after the 50 arrive you now have 170 on hand – more than the target. As a result, when you compare the actual on hand with the target you would not place an order that week. You would wait until the on hand inventory drops back below the target number to order another lot size of 50.

Adjustments to the Target Inventory

The inventory figures resulting from the formula provided are purely theoretical so a certain degree of management must be applied to them in order to bring them closer to reality. The first of these is an adjustment for anticipated changes in volume.

The weakness of this approach is that it is based entirely on the past, and the future may be quite different The resulting target inventory figures must be adjusted up or down in proportion to the degree to which the future will be different. If there is a reasonable forecast available the adjustment can be made on an individual item basis. However, as was discussed in Chapter 10, forecasting is inherently inaccurate for most items and it is usually more accurate to look at plans for item families, or other broad groups of items. If the overall plan for an item family anticipates an increase in volume of 10% over the next six months compared to the last six months, you would increase the resulting target inventory figures for all of the items in the family by 10%. This would enable you to plan on the variation rates from the past, but simply increment them up for future volumes.

The other typical adjustments are based purely on management and strategy. For a variety of reasons ranging from raising confidence levels that the company never runs out of a critical item, or never fails to ship on time to a critical customer, or to protect against risk, the target inventory quantities may be increased.

Risk adjustments typically include buffers for quality and delivery. If the supplier has a track record of quality problems then the target inventory may be increased either by a percentage based on historical defect rates, or by a lot size if the supplier has occasionally sent in defective lots. Adjustments for shipping delays or transit problems are occasionally made after the basic calculation, but are usually better made by increasing the lead times in the calculation. If the supplier is occasionally late on deliveries, adding a week to the planned lead time is typically the most appropriate way to adjust for this.

Although it is rare and should be a temporary situation, the inventory targets may also be increased to buffer for more serious risks – concern whether a supplier is financially viable, or for political instability in a supplier's country, or concern for a supplier located in a historically dangerous weather zone. In these cases the excess inventory may well be enough to cover the amount of time needed to find a new supplier.

Inventory Management
Normally it is sufficient to recalculate the target inventories on a quarterly basis, assuming the item is fairly stable and nothing significant has changed. However, the inventory planner must be particularly alert regarding new items and discontinued items. If the inventory targets are

117

not watched closely for these changes, new items will not be sufficiently available, and discontinued items will generate excessive obsolete inventory.

The advantages of this approach over item specific forecasting and MRP push planning are substantial. It relieves sales and marketing from detailed forecasting that consumes quite a bit of time while adding little value. In its place, however, it requires close communications between the people in sales and marketing and the inventory planner. Exceptions and changes must be quickly and closely communicated. Changes in the anticipated demand pattern for an item must be translated into changes in target inventory levels quickly, including new items, new customers, discontinued items, lost customers, customers switching from one product to another, and so forth.

While it is true that an ongoing dialogue between the people selling items and the people responsible for assuring adequate inventories is critical in any supply chain scheme, it is especially important in a demand pull application such as this. On the positive side, the only necessary ongoing discussion is for the exceptions and changes. For most items the system is very much self-controlling and self-regulating.

This self-regulating and very simple approach is the real advantage to such an inventory management process. Once the target inventories are in place it is very simple to determine when and how much to order. It is a 'sell one – buy one' or 'sell one – make one' approach and does not require extensive computer involvement or training. In many companies that deploy this demand pull concept with appropriately calculated target inventories the actual replenishment ordering and replenishment factory scheduling is relegated to people close to the item in the warehouse or on the factory floor. When the rules are simply to compare the on hand quantity with a target quantity, and place an order for the difference, the supply chain experts can negotiate a blanket purchase order that includes all of the necessary terms (i.e. price, lead times, lot sizes, shipping, packaging, etc…) and virtually anyone can be empowered to place a release with the supplier for the quantity needed to cover the gap between actual and target inventories. The purchasing people can then devote their time to more value adding efforts. The same is true with manufacturing orders. Blanket production orders defining lot sizes, routers, and Bills of Material can be set up, and virtually anyone can compare the actual on hand inventory with the target inventory and launch the process to make the appropriate quantity to cover the difference.

Finally, it is important to point out that, while our discussion has centered on finished goods inventory, the same analysis should take place at every level in which inventory is carried, based on the lead time from the preceding inventory.

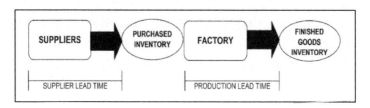

In analyzing finished goods inventory levels, only the production lead time should be included in the formula if there is an inventory of purchased materials from which production draws. Similarly, in calculating the necessary purchased inventory, the supplier lead time is used. Both analyses, however, are based on customer demand for finished goods. In the case of purchased inventory calculations, the amount of each item embedded in customer shipments by week should be used for the historical demand. In an MRP environment this requires 'exploding' the bills of materials for each items sold into its lowest level purchased items, and then summarizing all of the demand for each purchased item by week.

CHAPTER 20
Inventory Analysis and Make to Stock versus Make to Order
Decision Making

In the preceding chapter the statistical and managerial process for establishing demand pull inventory levels was discussed. The need for regular review was also explained – quarterly is usually sufficient for stable items; more frequently for items that are constantly changing. The most important element of that review is to identify anomalies in the data. The next chart indicates demand for three items, as well as the math for the Target Inventory formula.

In analyzing the data, the most important step is to look at the spikes in demand that create high levels of variability. In week 17 Item C had an abnormally high sales rate. Let's assume that upon investigation you learned that this was due to a one time order to stock a new customer's shelves. It is safe to assume that subsequent orders from that customer will fall into a more even demand flow in the future.

	ITEM A	ITEM B	ITEM C	ITEM C ADJUSTED
Week 1	58	312	100	100
Week 2	63	0	250	250
Week 3	28	0	275	275
Week 4	71	0	175	175
Week 5	44	0	225	225
Week 6	61	238	200	200
Week 7	60	0	250	250
Week 8	45	0	300	300
Week 9	37	0	250	250
Week 10	29	0	275	275
Week 11	54	466	275	275
Week 12	51	0	200	200
Week 13	12	0	325	325
Week 14	63	0	150	150
Week 15	51	42	150	150
Week 16	69	311	325	325
Week 17	65	0	1250	350
Week 18	42	0	325	325
Week 19	38	0	250	250
Week 20	55	0	275	275
Week 21	60	347	250	250
Week 22	48	0	325	325
Week 23	74	0	200	200
Week 24	36	0	175	175
Week 25	47	0	350	350
Week 26	39	0	200	200
TOTAL	1300	1716	7325	6425
AVG	50	66	282	247
1σ	15	138	207	67
2.2σ	33	304	456	147
Order Frequency	1	1	1	1
Cumulative Lead Time	4	4	4	4
Customer Lead Time	0	0	0	0
Target Inventory	115	674	1,194	541

Note that the raw data drove a target inventory of 1,194 units. When that anomaly is eliminated, however, the Item C Adjusted column indicates a target inventory of only 541 units – less than half. It is important to look at all anomalies and determine whether they should be included in the data set for determining target inventories, or if they should be excluded.

In this case, if Sales tells you that it was truly a one-time event and they do not expect anything similar in the near future, the 900 piece order should be excluded and the target inventory set at 541.

On the other hand, if Sales says they are working with other potential new customers and similar pipeline fill orders are likely to happen without additional lead time allowed, the target inventory should include the spike order and be set at 1,194.

This sort of analysis should include any item that experiences a substantial change in target inventory from the last review. It is important that such human judgment go into the process, and the target inventory figures are not simply automated and allowed to be set purely on the basis of math. The inventory levels are critical, and erring on either the high side or the low side can cause quite a bit of harm.

An analysis should also be made whenever there is an incident of a stock out. Perhaps the inability to ship is part of the <2% that is statistically unavoidable (assuming a 2.2σ planning figure), or perhaps it is the result of a one-time problem with a supplier or in production, or perhaps it is due to a one time large customer order that was completely unplanned. In such cases there is probably no reason to revise the target inventory level. If, however, it is the result of an ongoing change in customer demand, or it is the result of erroneous data in the set used to calculate the target, the figure should be recalculated.

The broader analysis of the target inventory calculation results are often policy decisions regarding which items will be kept in stock and which items will be made upon receipt of customer orders. Often this is not the result of analysis, but rather a strategic decision. Some firms have a business model that is built on having everything in their product list available for immediate shipment. It is not uncommon, however, to have a mix of stock and non-stock items.

Once the target inventories have been calculated (including any adjustments made for risk, quality, or any other management considerations), an analysis must be performed such as that shown in the figure on the next page.

At the bottom of each column are "Target Weeks On Hand" and "Target Turns" figures.

Target Weeks On Hand is the target inventory divided by the average weekly usage. For instance, the target inventory for Item A is 115.

This figure is divided by the average weekly usage of 50 to arrive at a Target Weeks On Hand figure of 2.3. This means that, in order to provide 98% on time delivery for this item, 2.3 weeks of inventory will be required.

	ITEM A	ITEM B	ITEM C	ITEM C ADJUSTED
TOTAL	1300	1716	7325	6425
AVG	50	66	282	247
1σ	15	138	207	67
2.2σ	33	304	456	147
Order Frequency	1	1	1	1
Cumulative Lead Time	4	4	4	4
Customer Lead Time	0	0	0	0
Target Inventory	115	674	1,194	541
AVG	50	66	282	247
Target Weeks On Hand	2.3	10.2	4.2	2.2
Target Turns	22.6	5.1	12.3	23.7

Further, dividing 52 weeks in the year by the Target Weeks On Hand figure (52÷2.3) yields a Target Inventory Turns figure of 22.6. This means that this item will, in theory, turn almost 23 times over the course of a year.

Clearly Item A is a good candidate for carrying in stock for immediate shipment. Because of the consistency of demand for the item, it turns quickly and requires minimal investment and minimal risk to provide a very high level of customer service.

Contrast those figures with the figures for Item B. Due to the very high rate of variability – inconsistency – in demand for the item, over 10 weeks of inventory will have to be held resulting in only 5 turns per year.

It is critical for supply chain and senior management to understand that these figures are what they are. Unless the rate of variability changes, or the cumulative lead time is reduced, there is no alternative to carrying the target level without sacrificing delivery performance.

It is often the case that a management decision is made to carry items with high Target Weeks On Hand levels – or low Target Turns – as make to order, while keeping those items with low turns in stock as available for immediate shipment.

It is important to understand that these figures speak to inventory risk, as well as financial investment and carrying costs. The risk of damage or obsolescence is much higher for Item B than Item A. Item B will sit on the shelf exposed to loss, theft, or damage for much longer periods of time. It also represents a substantial amount to have to write off in the event it becomes obsolete.

A final point from this analytical effort is that inventory reduction must come from changes in lead times and variability, and cannot be a function of managerial mandates or goal setting. All too often managers without an adequate understanding of the irrefutable statistical link between variability of demand, lead times and delivery performance attempt to reduce inventory by simply dictating that inventories be reduced by 10%.

As companies grow in their understanding that a consistent, level flow of products to customers has a significant impact on inventory levels and the cost of warehousing, they begin to question volume discount policies. Often customers buy in large, infrequent quantities rather than in a steady stream of smaller orders because of freight considerations. However, many times it is out of a misguided belief that large orders generate efficiency when, in fact, the opposite is true. In such cases, companies find that they are actually encouraging customers to buy at intervals and in quantities that drive the plant or warehouse to carry far more inventory than necessary.

CHAPTER 21
Lean Factory Scheduling Practices

The essence of Lean thinking on the factory floor is the continual improvement of the rate of flow. Tai'ichi Ohno, Toyota's former head of manufacturing during the period when the Toyota Production System evolved once said "*All we are doing is looking at the time line, from the moment the customer gives us an order to the point when we collect the cash. And we are reducing that time line by removing the non-value added wastes.*" While the time line Ohno referred to includes many aspects of the business beyond the actual flow of production in the factory that are beyond the scope of this book, the heart of that time line is the actual flow of materials into products. The principles for factory scheduling include three basic elements: Takt, Hiejunka, and Kanban.

Takt

Takt, or Takt Time, is the pace or rhythm of the factory. It is the speed of production, and it is a simple approach to synchronizing the rate of production with the rate of customer demand. Based on the German word, 'taktzeit', it literally means 'cycle time'.

The calculation for takt is:

Takt = Time available for production ÷ Rate of customer demand

For instance, if the factory operates eight hours per day, five days per week and the rate at which a particular product sells is 400 per week, then:

Takt = 2,400 (60 minutes x 8 hours x 5 days) ÷ 400

Or

Takt = 6 minutes

This means that in order to meet customer demand without building excess inventory, the factory should build one of these particular items every 6 minutes. Producing any slower than that pace will result in an inability to meet customer orders while producing any faster will create excess inventory.

Heijunka

Heijunka is a companion to takt, and it is the Japanese term for the concept of leveling production to meet takt. If the factory produced only one product then hiejunka would not be necessary. Level production would be the takt time. In the example cited previously, making one of that item every six minutes would constitute level production flow with no resulting excess inventory. However, because factories rarely produce only one item, the takt times for the various products must be blended. Heijunka is this process of blending takt times.

As the chart to the right indicates we will assume the factory makes three different products – A, B and C. The takt times for each product is shown.

In traditional batch manufacturing the plant would be scheduled to produce all of the Item A's needed, then change over to produce all of the Item B's, then the Item C's. Using hiejunka the plant

	PRODUCT A	PRODUCT B	PRODUCT C	TOTAL
Time available per week	2,400	2,400	2,400	2,400
Weekly customer demand	400	800	1,200	2,400
Takt	6	3	2	1

would produce a blend of the three items, with the blend based on each items takt time.

Leveled Heijunka flow

A B A C A B A C A B A

Traditional batch flow

A A A A A A B B B C C

As the chart above indicates, rather than produce all of each item needed in one batch, then switching over to the next item, the items are sequenced and blended to more perfectly meet demand with a level flow.

Kanban

The third Lean principle – kanban – was discussed in Chapter 15. The demand flow principle of kanban is simply the method for assuring that the next item is not produced until the previous item is complete. It keeps the hiejunka sequence intact, preventing excess material or excess production from accumulating in the event that an item is produced slower than anticipated or problems arise during production.

Practical application

Few plants, if any (including Toyota plants) actually achieve One Piece Flow (the term for the perfect combination of takt, hiejunka and kanban). The Lean concept of continuous improvement, as it relates to flow on the factory floor, is the continuous progression from large batch production to the ideal state of one piece flow.

This progression involves continually reducing the time increments required for the factory to produce some of everything. A typical manufacturing plant operating in a batch mode might produce some of everything every month. In a four week month, using the rate cited in the examples, the factory would spend two weeks producing 4,800 of Item C (one month's customer demand), then switch production over to produce 3,200 of Item B; and finally switch over to produce 1,600 of Item A. That way all of the necessary production would take place to meet monthly customer demand.

In this large batch mode, considerable inventory would be required. All of the customer demand for two weeks requirements of item A and more than three weeks requirements for Item B would have to be in finished goods inventory at the start of the month in order to be able to ship to customers while the plant is dedicated to producing the other items. (Or the plant would have to quote long lead times to customers due to the long time intervals until the next time an item group is produced.)

If the plant can reduce the size of its batches – say, by cutting them in half – and then produce some of everything every two weeks inventory levels and/or customer lead times can be cut proportionately. Under this scenario, the plant would only produce 2,400 of Item C before switching over to Item B, and so forth. The amount of inventory of Items A and B would only have to cover half as much time; or the customer lead times would be halved because it would only be two weeks until an item is in production again.

The factory's Lean progression – its rate of continuous improvement – is the rate at which it can continually reduce the time interval to produce some of everything. Many plants produce in increments of some of everything every two to six weeks. The better run plants produce some of everything every week. The truly Lean plants go beyond this, producing some of everything twice a week or even some of everything every day.

Of course there is no benefit to producing things in batch sizes smaller than customer orders. If customers want batches of ten, achieving one piece flow would not be practical. The plant should produce in batches of ten to synchronize with customer demand. It is often the *ability* to produce in lot sizes of one, rather than the execution of this that constitutes the objective of Lean Manufacturing.

The most common deterrent to achieving one piece flow through the takt-hiejunka-kanban process is set up or changeover times. If it takes an hour to change a machine over from producing one item to another then it is not economical to only produce a small number of an item. Traditionally, manufacturers have accepted this changeover time as unavoidable and a great deal of thought has gone into Economic Order Quantities (EOQ). EOQ thinking was an attempt to rationalize optimum production batch sizes while assuming changeover times were a static number.

Lean thinking is based on an assumption that set-up and changeover times can and should be reduced, and that producing more than the quantity needed to achieve takt time merely compounds the wasted expense of an excessive changeover time with the additional wasted expense of carrying inventory. A set of techniques referred to as SMED (Single Minute Exchange of Dies) is the Lean approach to reducing set up and changeover times in order to make hiejunka practical.

Note that the techniques address the wide range of set up and changeover situations, and that it is named for exchanging dies simply because its initial development and application at Toyota was to address the lengthy times required to change the dies in stamping presses. Quite often in manufacturing the changeover driving large batch size production has nothing to do with such tool changes. Instead the issue may be the amount of time it takes to change the fixtures and parts on an assembly line, or the amount of time needed to clean and recharge a continuous process making chemicals or food.

Regardless, the principles are the same, and reducing the time to switch from one product to another enables the factory to progress to shorter time intervals in which some of everything can be produced, in turn moving the plant closer to one piece flow.

On a final note, there are often drivers of batch production other than changeover and setup times. They might include quality concerns which drive the need to over-produce in order to have extra production in the event of defects, or batches driven by poor plant layout making it necessary to produce large quantities simply because it is not economical to move a small quantity of parts from one location to the location at which the next production step takes place. Lean Manufacturing shop floor techniques were all developed specifically to address the underlying drivers of the need to produce in large batches. It is a very common mistake for manufacturers to apply these techniques for their own sake, and not as part of an overarching goal to achieve small batches and move closer to one piece flow.

CHAPTER 22
Kanban and Demand Pull Execution

The term 'kanban' is a Japanese term meaning something close to 'display card' and was used to refer to the original demand pull concept developed and used very effectively by Toyota. Since then it has come into common supply chain terminology to refer to a wide range of demand pull methods, and it is this broader definition of the term that is being used in this book. Quite often the original Toyota system of cards serving as the signal to produce is the best one to use, but not always. The choice of signals is not important. What matters is the underlying principle of using a quick, simple communication mechanism to communicate when something has been sold so that a replacement can be made or bought.

Another common kanban signal is the container in which material is moved. Often called a 'returnable container' the concept is the same as the card system. The arrival of an empty container at the supplier facility or at a production operation is the signal and authorization to produce a container full of the same materials, parts or sub-assemblies and return it to the location that sent it.

There are many applications of electronic kanbans. These generally involve a computer, bar code scanner or Radio Frequency Information Device (RFID) reader at the location of use that automatically sends a signal to the location responsible for replenishment, where it can be displayed on any number of different devices, most often a computer screen or an electronic display board. The important aspect is that it be displayed in a manner that is widely and easily visible to the people in the area responsible for initiating the shipment or production necessary to fill the kanban requirement.

Although it is slower, it is often more practical for a factory to simply print a list of items shipped the previous day and have that list serve as the production schedule for the operation responsible for replenishing the inventory. In factories in which production occurs in weekly increments, rather than daily or hourly time buckets such as many Toyota plants, the kanban signal does not need to be transmitted immediately and a next day or even next week replenishment signal is sufficient. Of course, every factory should strive to continually shorten the scheduling and execution intervals as described in the previous chapter, which means that every factory should strive to get to the point at which quicker kanban signals are needed.

In Chapter 12 the genesis of kanban was described, where Toyota production leader Tai'ichi Ohno drew his inspiration from the manner in which milk moves through a grocery store. His mental image was of a string attached to a bottle of milk that a customer purchases and being attached all the way through the supply chain, pulling another gallon of milk all the way from the cow at the dairy farm to the grocery store shelf to replace it. It is this same mental image that should guide the development of any demand pull system. How it is done is not nearly as important as assuring it is driven by this idea of pulling replenishments through the entire supply chain.

It is important to avoid falling into the trap of believing there is only one way to approach kanban – the Toyota card method. In fact, there are an infinite number of equally valid possible approaches and the important thing is to develop and execute in the manner that works best in your specific situation.

Basic Architecture of the Kanban System

The first question is where the kanban signals must be created – how many kanban procedures are needed in the process? The following chart demonstrates the standard architecture, with a kanban signal between each operation, and from purchased inventory back to each supplier.

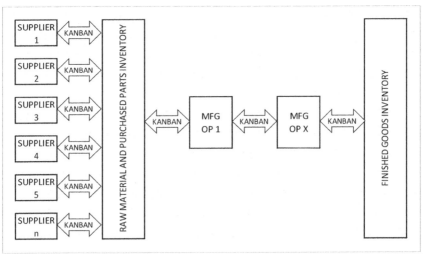

While there are situations in which such a comprehensive approach makes sense, in most cases it puts far too many kanbans and far too much work-in-process inventory into the process. The diagram below shows examples of two very common variations from this comprehensive approach.

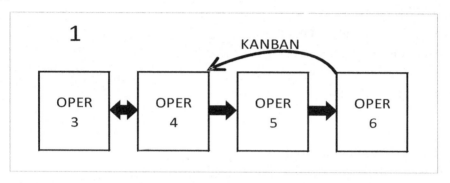

1.) Shows a kanban that skips over Operation #5 and sends a signal further upstream to Operation #4. There is no need for a kanban signal if:

1.   Operations 4 and 5 are in close proximity to each other.
2.   There is a fairly steady flow of the output from #4 through #5 (little or no work-in-process inventory between them).
3.   Operation #5 is not a constraint in the process.
4.   The production lot sizes for Operations #4 and #5 are the same.

These basic considerations should drive the architecture of the demand pull scheme in a production operation. The number of kanban procedures should be minimized because, while a simple manual demand pull system entails far less non-value adding waste and management time than an MRP based discrete work order process, the kanbans can also create wasted time and wasted effort, as well as work-in-process inventory. They must be maintained and controlled, and the fewer kanban procedures the better.

2.) Indicates a kanban directly from the production operation to the supplier, with incoming materials flowing directly to a point of use inventory storage area located near production. In fact, this is the preferred method of deploying demand pull with suppliers.

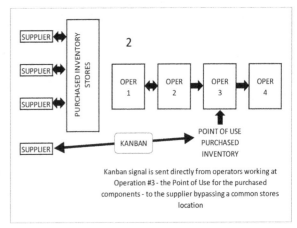

Kanban signal is sent directly from operators working at Operation #3 - the Point of Use for the purchased components - to the supplier bypassing a common stores location

In such a scheme, purchasing would typically have negotiated a blanket purchase order with the suppliers. That order would include all of the critical terms, including price, lead times, lot sizes and so forth. All that would be left to do is to send releases to the suppliers, advising them of the quantity to ship. When the materials arrive at the factory, they are moved directly to the production area's point of use location.

Note that such an arrangement does not preclude the normal receiving procedures, such as recording the receipt of the material for accounting purposes or any incoming quality inspection that may be necessary. It simply eliminates the steps of having to put the material away in a central inventory location, and then withdraw it when it is needed for production.

The primary advantage of this approach, other than streamlining and reducing the cost of material handling, is that the kanban signal can be released (typically in the form of a phone call, a fax or an email) by the production operators without need for dedicated purchasing personnel to be involved. Not only does it significantly reduce the workload for purchasing, but it puts monitoring and control of the materials in the hands of the production people who are closest to them. They know best exactly what is needed and when, and are usually better able to operate the kanban procedure to assure materials flow effectively. Having 100 production people who are each responsible for 5 parts – parts they see and work with every day – is usually much more effective than having one purchasing person attempting to stay on top of 500 parts – parts that are often not much more than numbers on a report or a computer screen to the purchasing person.

Kanban Quantities

The number of kanban signals for any individual part or product, and the quantity to be made or shipped for each kanban signal is the primary driver of the amount of inventory in the system. As a general rule, more kanban signals with smaller quantities to be made or shipped is better.

The simplest, but most inventory intensive, approach to demand pull is a two bin system. A two bin system is one in which there are two containers of parts, each with a quantity sufficient to assure adequate inventory over the course of the supplier or production lead time.

For instance, the plant uses 25 items per week, and the supplier has a two week lead time. The plant would start with two bins (usually the bins are actually the supplier's boxes) of 50 parts each. When bin 1 is empty, another box would be ordered from the supplier, the remaining bin (bin 2) of 50 parts would be sufficient to meet the plant's needs for the two weeks until the shipment arrived to replenish bin 1. At that point bin 2 would be empty so another order would be placed with the supplier to replenish it, and the plant would work from bin 1; and so forth with a constant rotation between bins 1 and 2.

If, instead of these two bins, the plant were to manage the part with three kanban cards (or any other appropriate kanban signal), and each card called for 25 parts, then the process would cover demand but with less inventory, as the chart below indicates.

As you can see, with the 3 card kanban system an order for 25 parts is placed every week while the two bin approach results in an order for 50 every other week. The two bin system settles into an average on hand ending inventory of 37.5, while the 3 card kanban approach generates on hand ending inventories each week of 25.

	WEEK 1	WEEK 2	WEEK 3	WEEK 4	WEEK 5	WEEK 6	WEEK 7	WEEK 8
Beg Inventory	100	75	50	25	50	25	50	25
Usage	25	25	25	25	25	25	25	25
Order	0	50	0	50	0	50	0	50
Receipts	0	0	0	50	0	50	0	50
End Inventory	75	50	25	50	25	50	25	50

Average inventory = 37.5

	WEEK 1	WEEK 2	WEEK 3	WEEK 4	WEEK 5	WEEK 6	WEEK 7	WEEK 8
Beg Inventory	75	50	25	25	25	25	25	25
Usage	25	25	25	25	25	25	25	25
Order	25	25	25	25	25	25	25	25
Receipts	0	0	25	25	25	25	25	25
End Inventory	50	25	25	25	25	25	25	25

Average inventory = 25

Of course there are other considerations besides inventory levels. The 3 card kanban requires weekly ordering and supplier shipments – twice as often as the two bin system. This means twice as much time to place orders and receive the materials. The more frequent shipments from the supplier may generate higher freight costs.

The appropriate kanban quantities require a balancing of these factors. In principle, more kanbans, each calling for smaller quantities, must be balanced with the cost and practicality of more frequent orders. Typically it is more practical to operate with multiple, small kanbans for production than it is for purchased items for the simple reasons that non-value adding accounting work and logistics costs are more significant with purchased items.

The other major consideration is the purchasing or production lot size. No kanban should be smaller than the lot size. In the example above, if the supplier lot size is 50 there is no benefit to implementing the three cards of 25 kanban approach. The order could not be placed on the supplier until two kanban cards totaling the lot size arrived at the trigger point.

The starting assumption for designing the kanban system is that there should be one kanban signal for each increment of lot size. For instance, if the total inventory required in the process is 200 items, and they are made or bought in lots of 25, then 8 kanban cards or signals should be created. From that starting assumption the number of kanban signals would be reduced (and the quantities each kanban signal calls for would be increased) based on economic and other practical considerations.

Managing and Controlling the Kanban Signals

In the preceding chapter it was stated that the number of kanban cards and the quantities each calls for is a function of the amount of inventory required in the process. In Chapter 18 we discussed inventory planning in a demand pull environment, and we explained the statistical and managerial basis for setting Target Inventory Levels, encompassing lead times, variability and so forth.

The results of that target Inventory planning effort determine the amount of inventory required in the process. If we were to go through that exercise and determine the Target Inventory for a particular item is 450 units; and if we were to analyze the process as described above and conclude that there is no reason why each card should call for any more than the production (or purchasing) lot size which we will assume is 25, we would create 18 kanban cards each calling for 25 parts to be made or shipped (450 ÷ 25 = 18). Those 18 kanban cards would be released to production and the system will self-regulate to assure constant pursuit of the target inventory quantity.

In Chapter 18 we also discussed the need to review and adjust the Target Inventory levels on a routine basis – at least quarterly and possibly even more often if circumstances require. Let's assume such a review called for a reduction of the target inventory from 450 to 375. This would mean that only 15 kanban signals are needed to assure constant pursuit of the new target inventory level (375 ÷ 25 = 15). The inventory planner would simply pull three cards from the kanban loop and file them away. In the reverse situation, if the review of target inventory levels dictates increased target inventory, the planner would create additional kanban signals and add them to the loop. The kanban system will automatically adjust in either case and assure constant pursuit of the target inventory.

If the kanban signal chosen is a physical object – cards, returnable containers, etc… – it is important that each signal be numbered. If there are supposed to be fifteen cards in the loop, the cards should be numbered 1-15. This will enable the inventory planner (or someone else) to occasionally audit the system to assure that no signals have been lost. Whenever the system relies on such a physical object there is always the danger that the object might get lost or destroyed. A kanban card could be inadvertently thrown away, or fall behind a desk or a machine. This would cause the process to contain too little inventory and create the probability of a stock shortage.

Kanban Signal Information

The information contained on the kanban card or signal should be kept to a minimum. The part or item number and description (often it is helpful to have a picture of the item, as well), the quantity to be ordered or made upon receipt of the signal, the location that is supposed to take action upon receipt of the kanban (production operation location or supplier name), the location the items or parts should be delivered to (along with the signal if it is a physical signal), and the work order or purchase order assigned to the task, along with the sequence number of the signal if it is a physical one (as described in the preceding chapter) are the standard elements of a kanban signal.

Additional information, such as work instructions, bills of material, quality standards, and so forth are usually best kept at the processing operation – either the factory production location or at the supplier

The kanban system should be kept as simple and visually controllable as possible. It is intended to be executed by anyone in the process with a minimum amount of training and knowledge of complicated supply chain procedures. Often kanban cards or returnable containers are color coded, and each area is assigned a color – red kanban cards or red containers go to machining; orange cards or containers go to assembly, etc... and each of those areas has a large sign indicating their assigned color. This way everyone knows where kanban cards should go, and it is easy to spot a card that ends up in a location other than where it is supposed to be.

CHAPTER 23
Mixed Make-To-Order – Make To Stock Pull

In many factories the challenge for production is to produce a mix of demand pull items for a make to stock inventory, and non-stock items that are made to order. What makes it challenging is in setting delivery promises for the make to order items in light of unknown capacity. Because kanban production is in response to actual customer demand, and that may vary from day to day or week to week, there is no way of knowing for certain how much production capacity will be available for non-stock items.

The most effective method of scheduling and controlling the factory in a Lean environment is what is referred to as a 'blue card – yellow card' system.

The starting point is to increase the target inventory levels for the stock items that are produced in a standard kanban or demand pull method. The degree the inventories must be inflated is a function of the expected variation on overall plant load. If the factory operates 80 hours per week (two forty hour shifts), but historical customer demand has ranged from a low 65 hours of production to a high of 92 hours of equivalent production (the amount of production that would have been required to make everything that was ordered by customers), then the target inventories for the kanban items would be increased by 15% (92 hours ÷ 80 hours).

Standard kanban items would continue to be produced with the same pull triggers – in many factories with blue kanban cards, hence the 'blue card' designation for the system.

As customer orders for make to order items arrive, the production information – item, quantity, work order, etc... along with routing information – the sequence of production steps needed to make the item completely - is written on a yellow 'kanban' card (it is not actually a kanban but is often called that simply because it looks quite similar and triggers production in the same manner an actual blue kanban card would). Those cards are released to production at the first step of the production routing.

The instructions to production are to work on yellow cards first, and then fill in the rest of the day with production from the standard blue kanban cards in the order in which they arrived. The work is then sent to the next operations where the same 'yellow cards first' rule is followed.

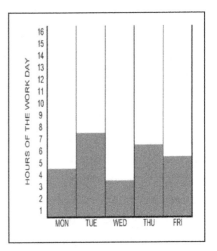

This method accomplishes providing very short lead times for make to order items, while leveling the workload on production.

Because the target finished goods inventory figures were increased, there is not an increased risk of missing customer shipments as a result of the plant not having sufficient capacity to produce all of the blue kanban requirements in a week in which yellow card (make to order) production is high. Weeks with high make to order demand will be balanced out by weeks with low make to order demand and the kanban system will 'catch up'.

When there are sub-assembly or sub-process operations – an injection molding operation that feeds into an assembly operation, for instance, multiple yellow cards may be issued. One card may go to begin the main flow to trigger production of the primary product flow, while companion yellow cards are simultaneously sent to injection molding and any other sub-operations in order to assure they are making the necessary components and sub-assemblies needed when the product reaches assembly.

Set-Up Optimization

Another typical variation on the Blue Card /Yellow Card method is one that takes into account optimum sequencing through a production operation – typically machining, stamping, or molding where set up times are a major consideration.

All of the items that can be produced in the area are analyzed to determine the most efficient changeover sequence. If the operation had to make some of everything, and the order in which they made them was entirely up to them, what order would they make them in?

That optimum sequence is reflected in a board with slots for the yellow and blue cards. As the example below indicates, the cards are not in item order, or production priority, but in the way that enables the most efficient manufacturing. As blue and yellow cards arrive at the production location, they are placed in the slot for the item number the card calls for.

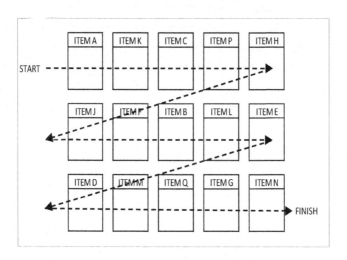

The scheduling rules for production are that they can (and should) produce in the optimum sequence, blending yellow and blue card requirements as long as all yellow cards are completed by a certain time – it can be by the end of the week if assembly will take place the following week; it can be by Wednesday if yellow card assembly takes place four days after receipt of the make to order customer order; etc…

The benefits to this approach are that (1.) it optimizes set-ups as much as possible; and (2.) there are often cases in which the same molded or machined component is used in both make to stock (blue card) and make to order (yellow card) end items. The weekly requirement for the component for all end item uses can be easily consolidated and it minimizes the risk of having to set up and produce the same item twice in a very short time span.

Chapter 24
Level Loaded Demand Pull Scheduling

Many businesses have a highly seasonal demand pattern that creates a major problem in balancing capacity with sales. Traditionally management of the supply chain in such conditions was seen as requiring a choice between problematic approaches: (1.) Flex the capacity up and down to meet demand; or (2.) Build inventory during the slower season in order to have sufficient product available when requirements exceed capacity in the higher season. Of course, the business could simply install capacity roughly equal to the peak demand, but that would result in substantial excess labor and cost during the lower demand periods.

Flexing capacity during the higher sales season entails the use of overtime, employing a temporary workforce or hiring employees, and then laying them off during the slower season. Each of these approaches has an obvious downside. Overtime carries a cost premium and risks driving employees too hard, resulting in increased mistakes and often higher employee turnover. This can be especially true when the peak season of the business corresponds with holidays or times of the year when employees prefer to use their vacation.

Temporary employees typically require extensive training, lower productivity levels and increased mistakes and defects. A planned pattern of hiring and laying off results in a continuous flow of less productivite new people and usually has a devastating impact on culture and morale.

Building inventory during the slower season is more often the preferred approach but it carries problems with it, as well. Such an inventory build requires dependence on forecasts – knowing what to build and how much in anticipation of peak season demand. Inevitable errors in forecast volume and mix cause the wrong inventory to be built, creating a need to work overtime, stretch lead times and miss delivery schedules during the peak period; and leaving unneeded inventory on hand coming out of the peak sales period that will sit on the shelf for a long time.

Demand pull strategies, such as kanban, have not been viewed as possible simply because there is no demand from which to pull when inventory is built in advance.

An alternative approach has emerged recently with very good results in highly seasonal businesses called "Level Loaded Demand Pull' (LLDP) that combines off season inventory building with kanban principles, relying heavily on the Blue Card/yellow Card kanban described previously. It should be noted that for businesses with relatively flat demand over the course of the year, the Blue Card/Yellow Card approach described in some detail previously is sufficient. LLDP is a combination of the Blue Card/Yellow Card method with rough cut capacity planning.

LLDP essentially creates an artificial demand, but uses demand pull principles to assure that the pre-season build is continuously balanced and that only the inventory with a high probability of moving quickly is built.

One Indiana based manufacturer in a very seasonal business routinely saw their lead times stretch out to 6 or 7 weeks during their prime selling season in spite of their using a forecast inventory build approach. After implementing LLDP they were able to ship their most popular times from stock upon receipt of order, and the rest of the product line within 1 week. At the same time average annual inventories dropped by 15-20%.

It can be a difficult concept to grasp, but the key difference between traditional off-season inventory build and LLDP is that traditional build has been aimed at forecasting and building a list of products ahead of demand, while LLDP is a process of moving hours from the peak period into the off season in a very dynamic fashion.

LLDP looks at the forecast in aggregate and is more concerned with the total hours of production in the forecast, and how much it exceeds capacity, and is less concerned with the specific item mix and quantities in the forecast. It also assumes that any forecast is generally more accurate for high volume items with fairly steady sales (even though those sales may well fluctuate throughout the year with the seasonality of the business), and less accurate for items with lower volume, more sporadic demand.

Classifying Items

The starting point for using LLDP is to analyze the demand frequency and variation described in Chapter 20. You will recall that the finished goods kanban quantity was calculated for each item using the formula:

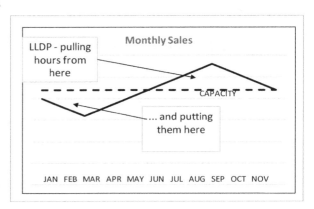

Average weekly demand

+

(2.2 Standard Deviations X (Lead Time Gap ÷ 2))

This kanban figure could then be compared to the average weekly demand to calculate the anticipated annual turns we can expect from an item when managed via a kanban or demand pull system.

The higher numbers in the Turns column indicate products with more stable demand. In the example Items A, D and F have consistent, stable demand and are, therefore, the best candidates for building inventory ahead of peak demand. The lower projected turns figures for Items B, C and E indicate more variable demand.

ITEM	Kanban	Weekly Avg Sales	Weeks On Hand	Turns
A	50	20	2.5	20.8
B	84	12	7.0	7.4
C	96	8	12.0	4.3
D	50	10	5.0	10.4
E	40	5	8.0	6.5
F	60	18	3.3	15.6

Where:
Weeks On Hand = Kanban ÷ Weekly Average Sales
Turns = 52 ÷ Weeks On Hand

The items with stable, less variable demand are candidates for pre-season build because they are 'safe' items. That is to say that if an excess of them are put into inventory they can be more quickly sold and the inventory reduced. The items with highly variable demand should not be built ahead of demand for the same reason. Due to their highly variable nature they may very well sit in inventory for a long time.

Typically something close to an 80/20 or 70/30 rule will prevail. A small number of items (20-30% of the total) will make up a large percentage of the total demand (70-80% of it). Regardless, it is through this analysis that the 'Blue Card' items are identified, and it is the same for LLDP. These Blue Card items will be the ones to build ahead of peak demand.

Defining Capacity

The next step is to identify available capacity per week for the period of time from the end of one peak season to the end of the next peak season. Capacity can be defined either in terms of labor hours or machine hours, depending on what determines the most severe constraint during the peak season.

In either case the same basic OEE (Overall Equipment Effectiveness) logic is used. This chart is an example of an actual capacity availability plan from a company that uses LLDP.

ITEM	Kanban	Weekly Avg Sales	Weeks On Hand	Turns
A	50	20	2.5	20.8
B	84	12	7.0	7.4
C	96	8	12.0	4.3
D	50	10	5.0	10.4
E	40	5	8.0	6.5
F	60	18	3.3	15.6

Where:
Weeks On Hand = Kanban ÷ Weekly Average Sales
Turns = 52 ÷ Weeks On Hand

Note that the holiday week of July 4 includes a plan to work fewer days. The critical point is to project the actual standard hours of production that can be expected in each week. In this example, they anticipate 24 people working 8 hours per day. They will lose 19% of the 8 hours due to paid breaks, safety meetings, and so forth. While they are actually producing they expect people to produce at 99% of the standard rate; and they expect a 95% quality yield.

143

In many cases users of LLDP will include lower anticipated OEE figures when they build in the productivity and quality losses they can expect from cross-training during the lower demand periods. Other times they will plan to shut down entire production lines or areas for a portion of the slower period and redeploy people elsewhere.

The important point to keep in mind is that the capacity projection must be a practical plan, based as much as possible on demonstrated results and reasonable improvement expectations, and not a theoretical capacity plan based on an assumption of perfection.

Quantifying Yellow Card Demand

Next we need to set capacity aside for anticipated demand for items we do not want to build ahead of the peak season – the Yellow Card items with sporadic, highly variable demand.

Recall that we view these items as inherently unforecastable due to their highly volatile nature. For this reason, rather than forecast them on an item by item basis, we want to forecast the total standard hours likely to be needed to meet demand for them in the peak season.

The best indicator of the total demand for such items is history, adjusted up or down for forecast changes in the overall business levels. Of course, if any specific information is available regarding these items that should be used. However most often we do not know with any accuracy which items will be ordered in what quantities. All we know is that there will be demand for them in aggregate, and that it is likely to consume capacity that we can estimate fairly well.

The standard hours for each Yellow Card item is multiplied by the actual demand for each comparable week last year, then adjusted up or down by some percentage based on our broader business outlook. For instance, we may think that sales for the product group in general will increase by 5% this year over last. We would then multiply the actual Yellow Card items sold for each week last year by their standard hours by 1.05. This would give us the capacity we need to 'set aside' for those items this year.

It must be clearly understood that this projection of Yellow Card demand is not a production plan, or master schedule. It is solely used to plan capacity requirements. The plan for the upcoming high demand season is that we will build the Yellow Card items to order. We only want to pre-stage inventory for consistently sold Blue Card items.

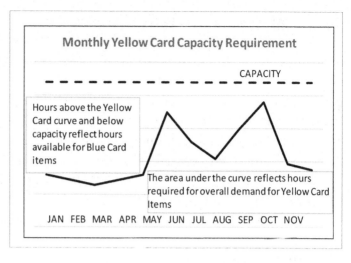

The capacity needed to be set aside for anticipated Yellow Card demand is then deducted from the total capacity hours available to determine a net capacity that can be used to produce the higher volume Blue Card items during the peak selling season.

You can see this basic calculation in the example below:

	WK END June 27	WK END July 4	WK END July 11	WK END July 18
Work Days	5	4	5	5
Hours per day	8	8	8	8
People	24	24	24	24
Utilization	81%	81%	81%	81%
Rate	99%	99%	99%	99%
Yield	95%	95%	95%	95%
OEE	76%	76%	76%	76%
Capacity Hours	731.3	585.1	731.3	731.3
Yellow Card Req	368.4	401.7	293.5	370.3
Net HRS Available	362.9	183.4	437.8	361.0

Smoothing Capacity Requirements

The next step is to plug production of the high volume Blue Card items into each week, calculating the hours of production they will require, and understanding that they will cause production demand to exceed available capacity. We will 'pull' production forward to balance capacity causing the pre-season inventory build to take place.

Note that a kanban quantity has been calculated for each Blue Card item based purely on demand. This true kanban quantity is the minimum level of inventory we will carry. As Blue Card production is pulled forward we are keeping an eye on these figures to make sure that inventory levels always equal or exceed the calculated kanban for each item.

If, for instance, the Blue Card production in the week ended June 27 requires 600 standard hours, and we only have 362.9 hours available after setting capacity aside for Yellow Card demand, we must reduce the production for the Blue Card items by a quantity needed to reduce Blue Card capacity requirements by 237.1 hours (600-362.9). When we reduce production of the Blue Card items that will obviously cause us to fail to meet demand and keep the kanban full. In order to remedy this, the 237.1 hours of Blue Card production must be plugged into earlier weeks in which we have excess capacity.

This smoothing by pulling Blue Card production hours forward continues until we have a plan that:

(1.) Assures adequate capacity during the peak season for Yellow Card items.

(2.) Produces enough Blue Card items to meet demand.

(3.) Does not cause any Blue Card item inventory to drop below the standard kanban requirement.

Note again that we have still not created a production schedule. These production calculations are simply for capacity balancing; and in the case of the Blue Card items used to calculate the artificial pre-season kanban levels. This graph shows how the kanban numbers have been artificially increased to plan for a pre-season inventory build.

We will look at the weekly ending inventories for each Blue Card item after the smoothing, and pick points roughly a month apart and use them as our new artificial kanban figures.

Even though the true kanban is only 24, we will introduce 68 kanban cards into the process in the month preceding June 20; then add four more cards to drive production to assure 72 units in the kanban by July 18, then pull 27 cards to assure the inventory drops to 45 by August 15, and so forth.

BLUE CARD		INVENTORY TARGETS		
ITEM	DESCRIPTION	06/20/15	07/18/15	08/15/15
1234	ITEM A	68	72	45

Management of the LLDP process

The advantage LLDP has over pre-season scheduled inventory build to a forecast is that it is still kanban driven. As orders come in throughout the inventory build period and into the peak season the plant is continually adjusting and building less of the items that are selling under forecast and more of the items selling over forecast quantities.

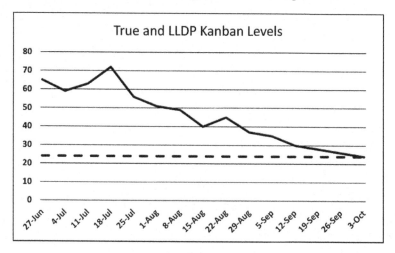

The forecast it relies on is not important at the discreet item level; only at the aggregate capacity required level. As a result of building only the items with steady demand, but having adequate capacity to quickly respond to orders with more sporadic demand, lead times are kept low and the inventory that is built will quickly sell. It virtually assures minimal inventory coming out of the peak selling season and is continually self-correcting for variations from forecast in volume and mix.

It is generally not necessary to re-plan and re-smooth weekly. Doing so would only introduce quite a bit of 'nervousness' into the system. Typically companies using LLDP will forecast and re-smooth quarterly for the first six months or so after the peak selling season, then as the next selling season approaches, begin re-forecasting monthly, and finally when they are into the selling season make weekly adjustments based on any extreme variations they are seeing in demand.

LLDP is not a technique for every manufacturer, but for those with strong seasonal businesses it has proven to be a powerful way to use the rapid flexibility of demand pull to minimize the negative impacts of the necessity of having to build inventory in the off season.

CHAPTER 25
Alternate Scheduling Approaches

While the takt-heijunka-kanban approach is the most effective means of assuring optimum flow in a repetitive manufacturing environment, a different approach must be taken in pure job shop environments. In job shop factories no product is exactly like any other. Heijunka is irrelevant when each product is unique, and the schedule is inherently a 'mixed model' schedule.

Traditionally there have been two basic approaches to job shop scheduling: backward scheduling and forward scheduling.

Backward scheduling is a straightforward process of starting with the date by which the product must be completed in order to meet the customer due date, then working backward through the series of production steps in order to determine the necessary start date for each step; and then backing the supplier lead times for each material item required at each step to determine the date each material item must be ordered from the suppliers.

Forward scheduling is the same as backward scheduling, only in reverse. It sets the schedule based on the idea that, if we place long lead time purchased material orders now, then a schedule can be established that results in making the product as soon as possible. Similarly, once the earliest arrival dates for materials is known, a schedule for each sequential step in the production process can be established.

The advantage forward scheduling has is that it enables greater direct labor utilization – people can be put to work as soon as possible regardless of the required due date. It is also believed to give the factory greater schedule flexibility. Since jobs are generally scheduled to be completed sooner than the customer needs them, it is not a problem to miss and reschedule any production step if needed as a result of a problem. Forward scheduling was the approach taken most often in the past but as manufacturers become more aware of and more driven by Lean Manufacturing principles they inevitably switch to backward scheduling. While forward scheduling may improve direct labor efficiency it does so at the expense of driving excessive inventory into the factory.

The 'water and rocks' diagram to the right is the classic Lean inventory analogy. Inventory is the water in the river that enables production to go on efficiently, keeping it free from the adverse effects of the rocks – in the factory those rocks might be poor quality or long machine setups among other things.

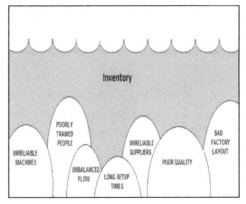

Lean is based on a principle of continually reducing the water level to expose the most serious problem. Factory scheduling should facilitate identifying and solving problems in the factory – not covering them up.

Note that backward scheduling can also include inventory buffers – putting water into the river to avoid rocks. The difference is that doing so in the backward scheduling process is a deliberate act – 'we are building an extra two days into step #4 because we know the machine used in step #4 is unreliable'. It is only prudent management to allow for such known problems while the factory works on solutions to its problems. This is quite a bit different from the forward scheduling idea of starting everything as soon as possible so we don't have to worry about whatever might go wrong.

The other major advantage to backward scheduling is that it creates focus on meeting customer requirements. Because forward scheduling is typically divorced from customer due dates it tends to create an atmosphere in which customer due dates are not important to factory personnel. It tends to create a culture in which direct labor efficiency is perceived to be a higher priority than customer satisfaction.

Note that both forward and backward scheduling have traditionally been 'push' techniques. Production is started and pushed to the subsequent operation whether that operation is ready for it or not. It is possible to execute such a schedule on a demand pull basis, and often this is the best approach.

An example would be a plant that builds custom trailers. Each trailer has its basic frame fabricated, and then the frame goes through a finishing process, such as anodizing. If the plant is making three trailers at once – Trailers A, B and C; and Trailer C is in the finishing operation, trailer B would be completely fabricated and sitting in front of the anodizing operation. Fabrication on trailer C would not begin until anodizing has completed trailer A and pulled trailer B into their operation. This sort of pull does not necessarily assure meeting customer requirements, but it does assure a wasteful build-up of work in process inventory does not take place.

More common is using demand pull for purchased materials and components, sometimes referred to as 'offset scheduling". The basic concept is quite simple: The parts for operation C are not ordered until operation A is complete (assuming the supplier lead time is equal to the production time required for operation B).

These techniques are especially useful in production operations that have a severe and consistent hard constraint. The Theory of Constraints is always useful, but on a practical level it is quite common to have three, four, five or more operations that are nearly equal in constraining the flow. To be sure, only one of them can mathematically be the constraint, but the others may be so close in terms of capacity relative to demand that the difference is negligible.

Perhaps more common are cases in which the constraint depends on the product mix. For instance, as long as the sales and production mix is 40% Item A and 60% Item B, then Machine X is the constraint, but if the mix changes to a 50-50% blend of A and B, then Machine Y becomes the constraint.

In these cases where there are practically multiple constraints, or shifting constraints with the product mix, scheduling with kanbans, or the Blue Card/Yellow Card method described in Chapter 21 tend to work best.

There are instances in which the production constraint is severe and consistent. It might be a particularly expensive CNC machine, or a paint or heat treat operation through which every product passes. In such cases, a push-pull approach works best. The diagram on the next page shows how such an approach operates.

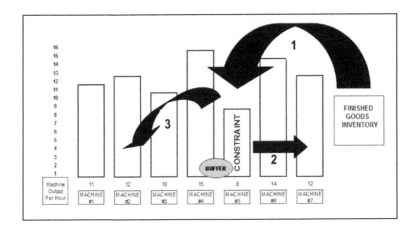

Arrow 1: A shipment from finished goods triggers a kanban signal. Instead of going to the immediately preceding operation – Machine #7 – the signal goes to the constraint — Machine #5. At the constraint, work is performed in the order the kanban signals are received, pulling from an inventory buffer at the constraint operation.

Arrow 2: The output from the constraint is then 'pushed' through the final operations to finished goods. The downstream operations – in this example Machines #6 and #7 – prioritize jobs in the order that the output from the preceding operation sends work to them.

Arrow 3: The buffer in front of the constraint is replenished through a straightforward demand pull process.

This combination of push and pull allows focus on the constraint. Often a supervisor or a scheduler is reviewing the kanban signals going to the constraint, intervening in the priority decision making process in a manner that assures optimum utilization of the constraint, while simultaneously assuring that production meets finished goods inventory replenishment needs.

The important principle to take from this is that production scheduling and factory flow must serve a number of important objectives: (1.) The most important objective is to assure that production occurs in time to meet customer shipment requirements, whether it is through replenishing a finished goods inventory or it is in producing make to order products in a one-off fashion; (2.) The scheduling and flow scheme must then maximize flow through the factory, leveling and balancing it as best it can, taking constraint utilization into account to the degree necessary;

and (3.) it must meet objectives 1 and 2 with the least inventory and the least handling costs as possible.

While demand flow is clearly the better approach to production scheduling system design, the most important principle is the application of sound logic in deploying an approach that optimizes each factory's unique environment. This can often call for a combination of push scheduling, demand pull or kanban processes, and the Theory of Constraints as described in the previous example. It is a mistake to believe that one and only one approach to factory scheduling and flow is universally correct.

CHAPTER 26
VMI, Consignment and Plant-in-Plant

There are a number of popular alternative supplier relationships that are aimed at tightening the link between the factory and its suppliers. They include consignment inventories, Vendor Managed Inventory (VMI) and Plant-in-Plant relationships.

Consignment Inventory

This is the simplest arrangement and it is a relationship in which the supplier maintains ownership of the inventory even though it is stored within the buying manufacturer or distributor's facility. Typically the buying entity does not pay for the material until it uses it. The primary benefit of consignment inventory is financial. The buying entity improves its cash flow and the inventory stays off of its balance sheet.

In the early days of manufacturing's understanding of Lean and the Toyota Production System when Just In Time (JIT) was viewed as the essence of the approach, many companies mistakenly believed that the idea was to minimize financial inventory. Consignment Inventory was an easy and popular approach to accomplishing this goal. Today most companies understand that simply shifting the ownership of inventory to the supplier does not improve the overall supply chain. The space, handling cost, and financial investment are not improved as a result of consignment inventory – merely shifted from the buying entity's books to the selling entity. It is inevitable that these costs are embedded in the total cost of the supply chain and no real improvement is possible.

Another, and more positive, application of consignment inventory is more often seen in the distribution process and that is the inventory risk of products with an uncertain market. A seller has a product that the buyer is not confident it can sell. Due to that uncertainty, the buyer is hesitant to invest in inventory and run the risk of losing its investment in the event that the market for the product does not materialize. It is often in the seller's best interests (with their inherently higher confidence level in their product) to assume the inventory risk and put the inventory in the buyer's distribution facility on a consignment basis.

This situation in the distribution model in which inventory risk is transferred back to the seller is also quite common in cases where the inventory is perishable. Food products, for instance, are often carried on a consignment basis where the seller takes it back if it has not sold by the end of its shelf life.

Outside of these specific inventory risk situations, consignment is only useful in assisting companies with cash flow problems. Even then, smaller shipments received more frequently are a preferable approach if the distance and freight costs between the seller and buyer permit.

Vendor Managed Inventory (VMI)

Vendor managed inventories are typically an extended version of the consignment inventory. It entails having the supplier not only maintain the inventory in the buyer's facility, but to provide overall management of the inventory, including restocking, record keeping and determining the appropriate inventory levels. It may include other services as well. Normally (but not necessarily) the inventory is kept on a consignment basis.

Vendor managed inventories are essentially a means of outsourcing some of the supply chain effort to the supplier. Normally it is used to manage "C" type items.

Note on inventory stratification: Inventory management includes a stratification aimed at separating the 'vital few' from the 'trivial many'. This involves separating inventory into class A, B and C items. A items are the 10% or so that represent the highest cost and/or the most technically critical items – perhaps those with the longest lead times. These are the few items that require the closest management control. The next most important items either from a financial or special control standpoint are the B items. Finally, the C items are the 70% or so of the purchased items that tend to be low cost and readily available. In terms of assigning purchasing and material control resources, the concept is to devote the most attention to the A items and minimal attention to the C items, with the B items falling somewhere between them.

Common applications of VMI are in the areas of fasteners, packing supplies/materials and printed materials. These tend to be low cost items that clearly fall into the C category for the buyer but are obviously very important to the seller. Vendor managed inventory arrangements benefit both parties because the buyer does not have to dedicate resources to managing a material category that often represents a large number of different items, but a very low financial value. The vendor is able to manage them better because of their unique knowledge of the items, coupled with the systems and processes they have developed internally for managing just such low cost items.

Another benefit for the seller in a vendor managed inventory arrangement is the opportunity to be inside the buyer's facility on a regular basis and see first-hand any opportunities to sell additional products. It enables the seller to develop relationships with people beyond the buyer's purchasing staff and learn where quality issues or material handling inefficiencies might be solved for the buyer by expanding the seller's product and service offerings.

Most important from the seller's standpoint, vendor managed inventory arrangements are a point of differentiation from their competitors. To the buyer, C items are often seen as commodities with little difference between the products sold by one potential supplier and another. Nuts, bolts and screws fall into this category. The provider of such items can distinguish themselves from other sources by including a service package that includes vendor managed inventories.

There is also a mutual benefit in the engineering and product design area that often is realized from vendor managed inventories. The buying company's design engineers are naturally experts in the critical technologies, features, and elements of their products, but they are not experts in the lower cost, lower technology items that are usually included in VMI programs. The engineer has their hands full dealing with core technology, for example, and has neither the time nor the knowledge to keep on top of new ideas say, in fasteners. The seller in a vendor managed inventory situation can fill that gap. Because the seller has a representative in the buyer's facility on a regular basis, it is easy for that representative to keep abreast of the product design efforts and suggest the best fasteners to use, thereby improving the product and expanding the seller's business at the same time.

Plant-In-Plant

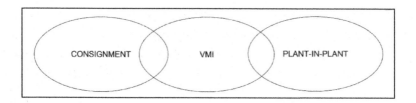

The next extension of the Consignment and VMI concept is for the supplier to operate a production operation physically inside the buyer's facility. It is really just taking consignment and vendor managed inventories one step further. A very common application of this approach is in printed materials.

Quite often printed materials are C items, costing pennies each, and are produced on very specialized equipment, outside the normal range of expertise for the buying operation. When the buying entity is buying in sufficient quantities to warrant it, the supplier will put a piece of specialized equipment in the buyer's plant and operate that equipment with its own personnel. In this arrangement, the seller realizes all of the benefits described in the VMI approach, while the buyer realizes the benefits of vertically integrated production without having to invest in the knowledge and technology.

Typical Examples of These Approaches

No two applications of these concepts are exactly the same. A good example of a vendor managed inventory in action is that of a fastener company and an electro-mechanical consumer products company. The manufacturer of the consumer products has placed a number of bright green racks in strategic locations throughout its factories. The color tells the employees that the inventory on those racks belongs to the vendor. The racks hold two large boxes of each of the various fasteners the manufacturer uses in the production areas adjacent to the racks.

Production employees go to the racks as needed and refill smaller bins they keep in their production area from the big boxes on the green racks.

Twice a week the vendor comes into the plant and replenishes any boxes that have been emptied since the last visit, and bills the manufacturer for the boxes that have been emptied.

In effect, the vendor owns the inventory on the racks, while the manufacturer owns the inventory that has been pulled from the rack and placed in the small bins at the production locations. It is a combination of consignment and VMI.

In another example, a printing company put a very expensive, flexible, high speed Xerox machine in an enclosed area given to it by a manufacturer. The printing company maintains electronic copies of all of the instruction manuals and other literature enclosed in the manufacturer's consumer products. The printing company maintains a kanban inventory of all of the different printed items, and production personnel pull what they need from the kanban at the printing operation.

The printer is responsible for operating the machine and providing all of its maintenance and supplies. It is up to the printing company to determine what machine to keep there and when to upgrade it. Once a month, the printing company bills the manufacturer for all of the literature that has been pulled from the kanban.

CHAPTER 27
Shop Floor Control & Cost Accounting Considerations

Shop floor control is the collection of activities involving reporting of production. It typically serves two masters: the need to know the status of production and the need to collect cost information. More and more often as manufacturers become leaner and the flow of materials from start to finish becomes faster, the need to track interim steps during production goes away. With many manufacturers, perhaps even most, the accounting requirements are the dominant driver of shop floor control activities.

To illustrate shop floor control considerations let's look at a simple production process involved in making a basic set of a table and two chairs, fully assembled and shipped in a single carton.

Table & Chair Set	Quantity	
Carton	1	
Carton insert A	2	
Carton Insert B	4	
Carton Label	1	
Table	1	
Table top		1
Leg posts		4
Leg post brackets		4
Leg post bolts		4
Leg post bolts		12
Chairs	2	
Seats		2
Legs		8
Leg brackets		8
Bolts		24

The factory has a table assembly area and a chair assembly area; and they both feed into a final assembly/pack operation.

The bill of material for the finished product is illustrated to the right. It lists all of the components parts, and is indented to indicate how the component parts flow into the chairs and tables, then into the finished product.

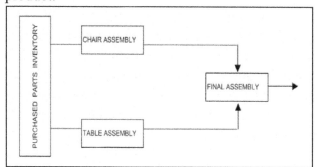

The production flow is shown in the chart to the left.

In a more traditional MRP type environment the chair and table areas would be likely to build to a work-in-process inventory that would be maintained in order for each production area to work at different speeds. The belief being that doing so enables the company to attain maximum labor efficiency.

Perhaps the table area can produce 20 per hour, the chairs can produce 50 (25 sets since there are two chairs per set) per hour, and final assembly can produce 15 per hour. Management would have the table and chair areas produce at a faster rate than final assembly can pack the tables and chairs, building an inventory of those components, in order to free the people in the table and chair areas to do something else. In the past the costs involved in carrying their inventory seemed to be more than offset by the benefits of being able to attain maximum utilization of the labor.

The Reasons for Shop Floor Control Activities

The primary purpose of the shop floor control function was to keep track of how many of each item – tables and chairs – were produced, and how much of each were in inventory and available for final assembly to use. It would also be used to establish production schedules for the table and chair areas, so they would know how many were needed to meet anticipated future demands.

Obviously this is a very simple example. In a typical factory there is apt to be an inventory of hundreds of different items. Even in this case, the table and chair assembly areas may be producing a wide variety of styles and colors, hence the need to keep track of their output and the tables and chairs available to package and ship the different models the company sells.

Increasingly, however, through the use of Lean Manufacturing techniques manufacturing operations are more likely to use a demand pull, or kanban, approach which diminishes the need for extensive shop floor control. Under such an approach, there would be a pre-set number of each table and chair established in the buffer inventory, and the production schedule for the table and chair areas would be simply whatever was needed to replenish the tables and chairs used in final assembly. Such kanban systems are typically controlled by cards or lists or simple, manual techniques on the shop floor and there is no need for anyone to report anything for production scheduling purposes. The inventory levels are preset, and there is always sufficient flow to meet demand.

Although pull systems alleviate the need for production control for scheduling systems, there is often a need to keep much of the shop floor control effort intact for accounting. In fact, in many companies the data collected for the MRP/ERP system is solely for accounting purposes and production has no need for it at all.

Accounting typically collects the shop floor information in order to compare the amount of labor and material that went into the various sub-assembly and assembly areas with the amount of production output. This calculation of labor and material cost per table and cost per chair is used in a variety of ways to track and measure production costs.

Shop floor control for accounting can get rather extensive. Because there are usually a number of different sizes and styles, each having different materials and each likely to have different labor requirements, an average cost per chair or cost per table is not very helpful. As a result, work orders (also called job numbers, production orders, or a number of other names) are created and used to collect costs. In this case, the shop floor control function is primarily work order control.

As an example, a work order may be issued to final assembly to put together 50 completed table and chair sets of a particular color and style. At the same time, a work order would be issued to the table assembly operation for fifty tables; and a third work order issued to the chair assembly operation to make 100 chairs. Materials needed to build the chairs would be issued from the purchased parts inventory to the chair work order. Materials for the tables would be issued from inventory to the table work order. Once work has begun, the people working in the table and chair areas would charge their time to the work orders in their area. When production is complete, the people working on the tables and chairs would report how many they actually made and the work orders would be closed. Accounting can then do its calculations of cost per table and cost per chair.

The tables and chairs would then be taken from the work-in-process inventory and charged to the final assembly area, along with the packing materials and labels, as well as the time the final assembly people spent on the order. They too would report how many they made and their work order would be closed. Accounting can then add their costs to the costs per table and chairs and determine a total cost for the finished products.

In a factory that produces unique projects – some capital equipment makers, for instance, that make major machines to individual customer specifications – each project would normally have a work order or cost collection number. There are very likely to be a number of subordinate work orders for the tracking of production, collecting costs and identifying the location and use of materials for various sub-systems or elements of the overall finished product. While the math is different – dividing the total costs by one rather than by a larger number of items produced in a batch or lot size – the intent and methods for shop floor control are virtually the same.

Issues and Considerations

There are a number of factors and concerns to be taken into consideration in determining the need and extent of the shop floor control processes. They all center on costs and benefits. Whether the tracking and collecting of shop floor production, time and inventory data is for scheduling, accounting or inventory tracking and control purposes (or usually some combination of the three) it takes time and has the effect of slowing production.

If a production person works on 8 different work orders per day, and it takes two minutes to clock in and out of each work order, the 16 minutes spent doing so each day represents 3% of that worker's 480 minute day. Looked at another way, the factory with 100 production employees has the equivalent of three full time employees doing nothing but clocking in and out of work orders.

This cost must be compared to the benefit management realizes from the data that shop floor tracking and control provides. Is knowing that this batch of chairs cost slightly more or less than the identical batch of chairs produced last week worth adding 3% to the labor cost of the chairs? Just as significantly, is it worth having the capacity of the factory diminished by 3% in order to achieve the detailed control the shop floor control system provides?

Quite often the answers to these questions is 'no', and firms conclude that shop floor data collection and tracking should be kept to a bare minimum.

Compounding the concern is the question of data integrity. There are companies in which the materials used or the products produced are highly susceptible to theft (a factory making jewelry, for instance), or the employees for some reason are highly prone to shirking their responsibilities (rare, but occasionally the case). These situations normally call for a higher level of tracking and control. In most factories, however, these are not major concerns. In most cases, the variances in work order costs – the chairs produced in one work order were $1 per chair higher this week than identical chairs produced last week, or the batch of 50 chairs that should have consumed 200 chair legs was charged with 250 chair legs from purchased inventory – the variance is not a real excess consumption of resources but an error in the reporting.

If people are 99% accurate in reporting their time, and the other 1% of the time they report the incorrect work order, write down the wrong time, transpose a digit in reporting production turning a '23' into a '32', then 6 employees working on 8 work orders per day are going to create 7 'variances' each week that are not really indicative of lost time (or gained time).

The same problem happens even more often with inventory accuracy. Companies with inventory integrity problems quite often find that little or no inventory was actually lost (and certainly no inventory was gained or came to be out of thin air). Instead, the problem with their inventory accuracy is entirely attributable to transaction errors. It is simple logic that more shop floor control transactions result in more errors. The time lost actually performing the transactions is compounded by management, supervision and support staff time spent tracking down the causes of variances to work orders and inventory records and correcting them.

The rate of errors and the amount of time lost to shop floor control is a function of the method. A very manual process – employees write their time and the work order number down on a log sheet, which is then sent to a clerical employee who enters the data into a computer – results in a larger number of errors, and a very low level of data accuracy.

At the other extreme – a bar code that registers employee identification and another bar code which identifies the work order while the computer registers the time the employee scanned him or herself onto and off of the job will be much more accurate. However, even an approach such as this is not completely foolproof. Barcode scanners make mistakes, and people scan the wrong bar codes. Also, automated approaches such as this have a cost.

Another issue to consider regarding shop floor control for accounting purposes is that of cause and effect. Tracking production, labor and material usage by job and calculating variances generally assumes that any variances have something to do with the job and this is rarely the case. A labor variance, for instance, might be the result of a poorly trained or new employee, or it might be the result of a machine problem that made it impossible for the employee to produce at the expected rate. The particular job the problem appeared in is pure coincidence. The machine ran slow on a job for blue chairs but would have run equally slow if the shop had been tasked with making red chairs.

There are many instances in which the need for lot control or the need for item control mandates that some shop floor control is an absolute necessity. Pharmaceutical manufacturers, plants making medical devices, systems and components for aerospace or the military, and a number of other industries have regulatory requirements to track and maintain records such as when batches of products were made or of which serial numbered components went into which serial numbered finished products. In such instances automating the shop floor control function is almost always the best course. Absent such requirements, however, the driving principle should be to minimize shop floor control efforts, limiting it to the collection of data that is relevant and useful for significant management decision making.

In the next chapter we will discuss the best approaches for shop floor data collection and control.

CHAPTER 28
Shop Floor Control Techniques & Technologies

Both accounting and scheduling needs dictate the necessity of some level of shop floor control and data collection. The type and amount of data, as was discussed in the previous chapter, should be based on a cost-benefit analysis. What will it take to collect the data and how accurate will it be (and how much additional work will be needed to audit and correct inaccurate data) versus the importance and relevance of the management decisions that can be made with the data. As was mentioned, given that data collection has a very real cost, and can have a sizeable negative impact of factory capacity and flow, data collection should be minimized to only that which is accurate and worthwhile.

Constraint Data Collection

In Chapter 16 we discussed the Theory of Constraints and in many operations (both factories and distribution centers) there is apt to be a major constraint that has a huge impact on the overall rate of output. In a factory this may be a particular machine, or in a distribution center it may be the rate at which a particular group of items can be picked for shipment. In such cases, the best course is usually to establish very effective tracking and control processes for activities at the constraint, and to largely ignore the details at the other steps in the process. If overall flow is not impacted by a variation in the rate of flow through the non-constraint steps with a fairly broad range, then there is little benefit to attempting to tightly control flow through those steps. At the constraint, however, if a minor disruption in flow results in a corresponding disruption in overall output, it is prudent to keep a close handle on the activities at the constraint.

Repetitive Manufacturing

In most factories where the same items are produced over and over there is not a regulatory requirement for detailed production tracking and control. It is also true in most cases that variations in cost from one batch of the product to another batch of the same product are either not significant or are not really a function of the item being produced, so shop floor control efforts should be minimal. The techniques best applied are (1.) backflushing, and (2.) input/output controls.

Backflushing

The premise behind backflushing is quite simple. If you made 50 chairs, you *must* have used 200 chair legs. It is impossible to make the 50 chairs with any other number. A positive shop floor control process that requires a person to enter onto a log sheet or into a computer the number of chair legs used only takes up time and opens the inventory records to errors. Instead, the logical and necessary number of chair legs is automatically deducted from inventory.

Using the bill of materials from the table and chairs example from the previous chapter, production would only report that they made 50 Table & Chairs Sets, then 50 times the quantity of each component required to make them would be automatically deducted from inventory – 50 cartons, 100 of carton insert A, 200 of carton insert B, and so forth through the entire bill of material.

Table & Chair Set	Quantity	
Carton	1	
Carton insert A	2	
Carton Insert B	4	
Carton Label	1	
Table	1	
Table top		1
Leg posts		4
Leg post brackets		4
Leg post bolts		4
Leg post bolts		12
Chairs	2	
Seats		2
Legs		8
Leg brackets		8
Bolts		24

The obvious substantial benefit from backflushing is the reduction of transactions from 15 (one for each item on the bill of material) to one. In this case, it results in a 93% reduction in time spent performing transactions and perhaps even more important, a 93% reduction in transaction errors that create inventory inaccuracies and create the need for projects to identify variances, along with their causes and what actions to take in order to clean up the data.

The only additional data collection requirements in a backflushing environment are for exceptions – usually related to quality issues. If, for instance, a hole is drilled wrong on one of the leg brackets, and an additional leg bracket must be withdrawn from the purchased parts inventory to replace it, a transaction to record the scrap and relieve inventory of one more leg bracket than the production order would have normally required is necessary. In Chapter 21 we will discuss quality control matters in more detail, however, regardless of the decision to use backflushing, an event requiring scrapping an item will inevitably result in additional transactions and record keeping, so backflushing does not really expose the factory any more than any other scheme to potential inventory inaccuracies as a result of scrap.

The negative aspect of backflushing that arises in plants that carry an excessive level of work in process inventory is the difficulty that it can present in taking a physical inventory. If the factory has to conduct an annual physical inventory, products on the shop floor in various stages of production must each be looked at individually to determine exactly which components are embedded in them at the time of the inventory. The components must then be manually deducted from the on hand records of material in the purchased materials inventory, and then the actual quantities in that inventory can then be compared to the records less the manually deducted portion. This can be very time consuming, and backflush operations always find it expedient to try to clear the production floor of work in process as much as possible prior to conducting a physical inventory in order to minimize this.

It should be noted that backflushing is just as useful in distribution center operations too. Rather than one transaction to record picking an item from the shelf for a customer order, and then another transaction to record actually shipping the order, it makes sense to simply record shipping the order, and automatically deduct the items on the order from the on hand shelf inventory. Again, the only additional transactions would be to record the things that went wrong. If an order is shipped short, for instance, with one or more items on the order placed on back order or canceled, that must be recorded; or if an item is substituted on the shipment, then the backflush transaction must be corrected to reflect what actually happened.

Input/Output Control

	Quantity	Labor Hours
Table & Chair Set		0.2
Carton	1	
Carton insert A	2	
Carton Insert B	4	
Carton Label	1	
Table	1	0.4
Table top		1
Leg posts		4
Leg post brackets		4
Leg post bolts		4
Leg post bolts		12
Chairs	2	0.6
Seats		2
Legs		8
Leg brackets		8
Bolts		24
TOTAL		1.2

Instead of detailed tracking on an order by order basis to monitor labor performance a better approach is usually to adopt basic input/output control. This is simply calculating the total labor that went into production compared to the labor value of the total amount that was produced.

The companion to the bill of material is a routing record that indicates the steps in production, and it would normally include the standard labor needed to produce the product on the bill of material. The record above shows that it takes a total of 1.2 standard labor hours to make our completed table and chair set.

If we were to record production of 50 table and chair sets, we should have consumed 60 labor hours (50 sets X 1.2 hours per set = 60 total hours).

The total labor hours 'earned' by production for the day, the week or the month are added up – the 60 hours for this product plus similarly calculated hours for all of the other products the operation completed. This total is then compared to the total hours worked. If there were ten people working making tables, chairs and completed assemblies, and they all worked forty hours, then the 'Input' figure would be 400 hours (10 people X 40 hours each = 400 Total hours of input to the operation).

The 400 hours of Input would be compared to the 390 hours of Output as shown on the figure below.

	Quantity Produced	Standard Hours Each	Total Earned Hours
Table & Chair Set - Blue	50	1.2	60
Table & Chair Set - Red	75	1.2	90
Table & Chair Set - Green	25	1.2	30
Table & Chair Set - Orange	40	1.4	56
Table & Chair Set - Yellow	50	1.4	70
Table & Chair Set - White	60	1.4	84
TOTAL Earned Hours			390

Input/Output control, as opposed to specific lot by lot tracking and control is based on the valid assumption that any variance is not a function of the particular item being produced but, more likely, something related to the people or machines being used. The variance can just as easily be manifest on any one product as another.

If management believes that the variance – in this case the ten hour difference between the 400 hours input and the 390 hours output – is significant, the total variance can be explored and the cause determined. Most often the cause is already well known by production leadership. Again, the value of Input/Output control as opposed to order by order tracking and control is a significant reduction in both time lost to data collection and exposure to errors.

Lot and Item Control

In cases in which item and/or lot number control is necessary, the driving principles must be to minimize and automate. Having production personnel manually log data, then passing it on to someone else for entry in a computer is obviously far less efficient than simply having a computer terminal on the shop floor and having production personnel simply enter the data themselves. Less time lost and halving of the exposure to errors are the clear advantages.

While it widely varies between people and operations, there is no doubt that manual data collection is far less accurate than automated data collection. Bar code systems are typically 98%+ accurate while manual efforts are often 90% accurate or less. If the collection of the detailed shop floor data is important enough to warrant the time and expense needed to do so – in a regulated environment or one in which the material has a very high intrinsic value, for instance – then it should warrant an investment in basic bar coding technology. In such applications, all of the data – item numbers, order numbers, time, and employee identification should be scanned from a pre-printed bar code.

A great deal of diligence must be taken in developing the system to identify potential errors and effective checks must be built into the system to preclude them. Examples might be to compare materials with bills of material to prevent anyone from charging material to an order that is not on the bill, or to prevent anyone from charging materials twice, requiring manual intervention when someone attempts to scan material to an order that has already been scanned. There is an old adage that automating anything often results in the ability to generate and communicate bad information at speeds you never before thought to be possible. It is very true.

In highly automated operations or in those in which the customer is mandating the application of RFID (Radio Frequency Identification) chips in the products, the use of scanners to track production and components by RFID is an even better approach. The same admonitions apply, however, and a great deal of care should be taken to assure that bad data is not picked up by the RFID shop floor control system.

Blanket Production Orders

Another valuable source of streamlining and simplifying shop floor control is the use of blanket production orders. If the plant produces Blue Table and Chair Sets over and over, there is often little or no value in creating and collecting data to a unique work order each time they are made. A much better approach is to create one order for the Blue Table and Chair Set finished item with an order quantity sufficient to cover all of the sets that might be made over the course of the year, then to track all data to that same blanket production order, closing out the order at the end of the year for whatever quantity has actually been produced over the year.

While the use of blanket work orders takes away the ability to track cost variances from one lot of production to the next, as was discussed, such variations are most often unrelated to the order and have more to do with issues inherent in the production process. When the plant

170

has converted to backflushing and Input/Output controls then the use of blanket orders is a natural next step.

Summary

The more traditional approaches to shop floor control – the creation of individual work orders and tracking each item of material used and each person's labor – results in a great deal of plant inefficiency and exposes the production, inventory, and accounting system to a great deal of error, which in turn requires even more inefficiency to run down and clean up. Such detailed shop floor controls should only be used when there is a compelling business reason for doing so.

The best practices for shop floor control are the Lean approaches of backflushing, Input/Output controls and the use of blanket production orders. Where detailed control is necessary – due to regulatory requirements, inherently valuable materials or the need to closely manage a constraint – the shop floor control function should be automated as much as possible.

Note that transaction intensive shop floor controls or the leaner approach are not an either/or proposition. If the plant has some compelling reason to track some material items individually, the rest of the items on the bill of material can be transacted through backflushing. Similarly, the need to maintain lot or serial number controls does not necessarily mean that labor cannot be managed through Input/Output controls. It is only when there is a compelling requirement to create a record of exactly who worked on which product that Input/Output controls are not applicable.

Overall, the driving principle in shop floor control should be simplicity and minimization.

CHAPTER 29
Purchasing Practices and Execution

Traditionally, supplier-manufacturer relationships have been adversarial ones. Often they are friendly enough, but they have centered on tension over pricing, lead times, and other terms of the supplier-purchaser relationship. The idea has been to treat the relationship as something of a zero sum game. If we can get lower prices that will translate directly into higher profits; while the supplier is driven by the same idea – if he can get higher prices then he will be that much more profitable.

Suppliers As Partners

The idea of supplier partnerships is an appealing one. Everyone would like to have their suppliers partner with them in pursuit of their objectives but that is not easy. The question is why would a supplier want to do this? The dictionary definition of partnership is, *"A relationship between individuals or groups that is characterized by mutual cooperation and responsibility for the achievement of a specified goal."* The rub is that "specified goal". Your goal is maximizing your profits, while the supplier's goal is to maximize his. Where is the incentive for either of you to mutually cooperate or to accept mutual responsibility for the other one's goal? It is hard to see any reason to do so; hence the tension in the relationship as each of you looks to the other for support in achieving your own goals.

In fact, the mutual goals are not that difficult to define in a Lean environment. The mutual financial objective is not to optimize each party's profit, but to eliminate the non-value adding waste in the combined effort. The other terms of the relationship – lead times, quality requirements, etc… are defined by the supply chain in which you and your supplier participate and, as such, are not something for either of you to negotiate for individual advantage.

The tension comes from an over-simplified understanding of the economics of both your and your supplier's businesses. The traditional view has been that businesses operate on the simple equation:

Cost + Profit = Price

Your supplier is most likely driven by some version of the full standard cost for the product he is trying to sell you. He views that cost as a somewhat static figure and is trying to get the highest price for that product above that standard cost in order to maximize his profit.

You are driven by the same equation, but your idea is that the price you get from your customer is a somewhat static figure, so if you can negotiate a lower price from the supplier it will translate into a lower overall cost for your products and more profit for you as a result.

That logic is true enough, but it misses the basic economic theory of Lean Manufacturing. Lean is driven by a subtle but significantly different version of that equation. Which is:

Price – Profit = Cost

The idea is that the price is not up to either you or your supplier, but is instead set by the end customer in the supply chain. If you are making hammers, for instance, and selling them to The Home Depot, the pricing is not something you control, or even something The Home Depot controls, but is determined by the guy who walks into a Home Depot store to buy a hammer. That person could care less about The Home Depot's cost or profits, or yours, or the supplier who sells you handles for the hammers you make. His only concern is the value of the hammer relative to the price he is being charged.

If you are buying handles for $2 and selling finished hammers to The Home Depot for $8, and they are in turn selling them for $10, your only basis for demanding lower prices from your hammer handle supplier is if the final customer will no longer pay $10 and demands something lower. Your supplier's only basis for demanding higher prices is if that end customer becomes willing to pay more for the hammer.

The question is not either your or your supplier's total cost, but rather, what is the amount of value that each of you add? If you and your supplier can collaborate and figure out how to make a hammer with a better handle, and that translates into a hammer the end customer will pay more for, so much the better. This process will be discussed further when we get to product development. More often though, the matter is reducing the cost in the supply chain.

The principle behind the Lean 'Price – Profit = Cost' equation is that neither you, your supplier, nor your customer controls the price. As was stated, that is set by the customer at the end of the supply chain. Profit is not particularly negotiable either. You, your supplier, and your customer need to make a profit, and whatever profit there is must be shared proportionate to the amount value that each adds to the final product.

What each participant in the supply chain does control is their cost. It is in no one's interests to reduce the value of the final product – to reduce costs by making hammers that have lower quality, less utility, or less reliability for the end customer. That leaves the elimination of non-value adding costs as the source of higher profits.

Both you and your suppliers incur a lot of costs that do not add to the value of the material they sell to you or to the cost of the products that you sell down the supply chain. Those costs are likely to include such things as inventory related expenses, such as material handling, floor space costs, inventory transaction expenses, and so forth. You probably have costs related to quality, including the cost of inspectors, documentation, sorting, rework and scrap. You both have administrative costs – sending and paying bills, sending and processing purchase orders, and you have freight and logistical expenses. There are probably many more such non-value adding expenses that both you and your suppliers incur. None of those expenses make the end product any more valuable.

The goal you and your supplier must mutually agree to achieve is the reduction of each other's non-value adding expenses. How can you improve the relationship to reduce those costs? The $2 price of the hammer handle should not be the source of conflict, just as the $8 price you charge The Home Depot is not something to spend much effort on increasing. Instead you and the supplier should focus on increasing both of your profits by eliminating the waste you both incur. This is the essence of the partnership principle.

Supplier Selection

It can be fairly said that the best way to gauge a company's supply chain is to look at its suppliers, how they were selected and how the

	Poor Practices	Best Practices
Supplier Selection Criteria		
Price	90%+ of the selection criteria	One criteria of many
Supplier Quaity System	Not considered	Critical
Supplier Capacity/Lead Time	Rarely considered	Critical
Supplier Technical Capability	Not considered	Could be critical
Supplier Financial Strength	Not considered	Critical
Supplier's Strategy	Minimal	Significant
Supplier Risk Profile	None	Important
Use of Reps & Distributors	Frequent	Rare
Competitive Concerns	Little	Significant
Purchasing Process		
Pricing	Quote Each P.O.	Long term contract or P.O.
Transactions	Send P.O. for each delivery	Minimal documentation
Relationship	Personal	fact based
Relationship		
Involvement in New Products	None	Extensive in some cases
Knowledge of Your Strategy	Suppliers are told little	Suppliers well informed
Breadth	None beyond buyer & sales rep	Extensive in some cases

company interfaces with them. The following indicates the typical extremes between new and poorly run companies, and the best companies in terms of their supplier relationships:

The evolution of a company in terms of its supply chain execution is largely a reflection of a broadening of its understanding of the total economics of the supply chain. The supplier selection process should reflect this.

Suppliers can be broadly grouped into three basic categories:
1. A few critical sources for the materials and components that constitute the heart of your product's cost and value.
2. A large number of suppliers who provide the basic materials you need. Their products are not particularly unique, but collectively make up the bulk of your products.
3. Those viewed as "C" items, or commodity providers. The high volume, low cost ancillary pieces you don't view as critical but, nonetheless, must be bought. Typically Maintenance Repair and Operations (MRO) suppliers are also included in this category. These are the people who provide the various supplies you need that are not part of

the products, but are necessary for the ongoing operation of the business.

The category one suppliers – those critical to your product – should be selected strategically. Their technical capability, quality levels, willingness to work with you, alignment with your strategic objectives and managerial competence are more important in the long term than their immediate pricing.

The selection of these suppliers is a much broader proposition than simply having purchasing people solicit quotes and perform a perfunctory evaluation of them. Senior leadership and the firm's technical experts must play a role in evaluating them. Just as important as their product and process technology is their interest in working with you in pursuit of your long term objectives. Typically, the supplier evaluation is a broad, company-wide project and the relationship with such suppliers is more comprehensive than mere purchasing. Your technical people will have relationships with their technical people; your financial people will have relationships with theirs, and so forth.

Category 2 suppliers should be selected on the basis of:

1. Price – Are their prices competitive and do they have the willingness and ability to work with you in the manner described previously in an ongoing effort to eliminate non-value adding waste?
2. Quality – Whether they have a formal process of quality control, and an ongoing process of quality improvement.
3. Delivery and Lead Times – Whether they have a level of supply chain sophistication that assures they understand the critical nature of lead times and can meet the lead time requirements necessary for you to achieve necessary flow through your business.

In addition to these basic business criteria, these suppliers are the subjects of the strategic criteria described in Chapter 4 and throughout Section I in which company strategy was discussed.

These suppliers are typically subject to an evaluation process that includes looking at such criteria as:

- The nature and effectiveness of their quality system
- The nature and effectiveness of their production and inventory planning and control processes – do they have processes that lead you to believe they are sufficiently under control to meet their delivery promises?
- Their financial stability
- Their commitment to continuous improvement – can they work with you on non-value adding cost reduction efforts?
- Their compliance with ethical, environmental and other social concerns – obtaining Country of Origin certification is usually part of this
- Their capacity availability and planning – can they meet unexpected surges in your levels of demand from them?
- Their geographic location – this will be discussed further in the next chapter, but an important consideration is how the supplier will fit into your overall freight and logistics scheme
- Risk factors and their contingency plans – are they subject to a high level of geographic (weather related or logistical) risk? Labor problems that could impact their production? Political and economic risk? Included in this evaluation are looking into where their own suppliers are located and the degree of risk they might incur as a result.

Finally, the category 3 suppliers – "C" level items, commodities and MRO items. This is typically more of a purely price driven exercise, however, it is often an area in which there is not much price differentiation between possible suppliers and the selection should be based on the supplier's willingness and ability to deliver in a manner that reduces your non-value adding costs. These suppliers are often the candidates for Vendor Managed Inventories and Plant-In-Plant arrangements.

Terms and Arrangements

For the same reasons discussed previously, supplier lead times and quality requirements should not be subject to much negotiation or controversy. Just as the pricing is set by the supply chain, so are lead times and quality requirements.

If your customer requires two week lead times, then your suppliers should be expected to do the same or less. If you have two week lead times, and your supplier demands four week lead times, we have seen how this translates into greater inventory investment demands on you. This means you are taking on a disproportionate investment and risk level. Of course, the inverse is also true. If your customer requires two week lead times, then for you to impose one week lead times on your supplier would mean expecting that supplier to essentially finance a portion of your business.

This is not to say that, if a supplier can deliver in shorter lead times they should not be asked to do so. Nor does it mean you should not work with suppliers to continuously reduce their lead times. Rather, it means you must recognize that a supplier who provides shorter lead times than your customers require is contributing to the reduction of your overall costs, and the prices you are willing to pay should reflect that contribution.

Quality terms should be based on the same principles. If the end of your supply chain is a Walmart store where customer returns are allowed without explanation and full credit is given, those harsh quality terms should rightfully be imposed all the way back through the supply chain.

The point is that the terms you impose on your suppliers should be the same as those imposed on you from further down the chain. If the supplier cannot meet those terms and conditions, you may still want to deal with that supplier, but your pricing should reflect the fact that they are imposing their share of the cost of complying with those conditions on you. Likewise, if your supplier goes beyond those terms and conditions, you should recognize that in doing so, they are potentially contributing to a reduction in your non-value adding expenses and they should be rewarded appropriately.

On a final note, we previously described the use of long term blanket orders as a very effective means of streamlining and hurrying along the buying process. This is a very common Lean approach to purchase execution. From the supplier's perspective, this practice can go a long way towards assisting in reducing the lead time to you. When suppliers quote long lead times there is always an underlining constraint that drives them to do so. Perhaps it is a physical capacity constraint and it is tough for them to take on the risk of investing in new equipment without assurance of future business that will enable them to get a return on that investment. Perhaps it is because they, in turn, have to buy raw material that has a long lead time and is only used in their product, and they are reluctant to make that investment and risk being stuck with the material if you don't buy it. Regardless of the cause, issuing long term contracts and blanket purchase orders can go a long way toward making it more feasible for your suppliers to meet necessary lead time objectives without creating much increased risk for you.

Similarly, Electronic Data Interchange (EDI) is a streamlined purchase execution technique. It essentially means placing orders with your supplier automatically – from your computer directly to your supplier's computer – without the need for much human intervention or physical paperwork.

These are techniques that get to the heart of the mutual effort to eliminate non-value adding expenses. That mutual commitment to common objectives is what drives both you and your supplier to work towards developing techniques such as these that make the purchasing process more seamless.

CHAPTER 30
Integrating Logistics & Freight

An independent trucker – one person owns and operates the truck as an independent business person – typically works through brokers. The brokers sell trucking services, and then sub-contract the work to an independent trucker. The independent trucker might get a contract to carry a load from Los Angeles to Dallas; and then he looks for the broker to find another load for him originating as near to Dallas as possible. He usually doesn't care where that load goes, so long as he is confident there will be another load nearby. If he has to drive empty at his own expense for long distances then he is not making any money, but he still has to pay for gas, his time and the cost of the truck and trailer. The independent trucker worries about time as well as distance. If he has to stop often to load and unload partial truckloads, again he has to worry about paying for his time and the cost of the truck.

Brokers have contracts with lots of truckers and, when you call them to arrange for shipping, they look over their network and try to find one of their sub-contract drivers who will be near you and arrange for that driver to haul your load.

Big trucking firms operate in almost the exact same manner. The difference is that the drivers are employees, and the act as their own broker. The economics, however, are the same. They worry about time (the cost of the driver and the truck) and distance (the cost of the fuel). In all cases the truckers are keenly aware of the fact that filling the truck as much as possible leverages all of their costs to the greatest degree.

In light of the time, distance and volume drivers of freight costs, managing your freight is largely an exercise in network optimization.

A factory or distributor in Arkansas with 12 suppliers has a number of options in managing the inbound freight network. The least efficient is that in the map to the previous page, where each supplier is treated as an independent node, shipping independently. That factory is more likely to have to bring more material in than it really wants in order to keep freight costs from becoming prohibitive.

On the other hand, if the factory were to look at the complete supplier base as a network, there are possibilities to link suppliers into an efficient sequence based on geographic proximity and volumes, then possibilities start to emerge for improving the supply chain flow without much increase in freight expenses.

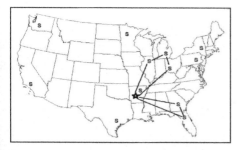

Instead of treating the three suppliers in Illinois, Michigan and Ohio as separate entities and looking for the best freight rates for each of them, they can be combined into a 'milk run', with a truck dedicated to making a weekly run from the factory to the Illinois supplier, then to Michigan, then to Ohio, and back to Arkansas.

As independent entities, the economics of freight would drive the company to ship full truckloads from each supplier once a month. As an integrated network served by a milk run, each supplier can ship a week's worth of material. Inventory is lower, because (referring back to the inventory logic in Chapter 17) with weekly order frequency intervals, and weekly inbound shipments, the amount of inventory needed to protect against variations in demand from one shipment to the next is lower.

The increase from three freight hauls per month to four will not actually be significant, if it increases at all, when the freight contract is given to a local, independent trucker. He would set lower rates because he knows he has an assured, regular route. Were he to operate independently through brokers, he would have some degree of empty back hauling as he goes from one job to another. An allowance for this empty back hauling would no longer have to be a part of his pricing. He would also be willing to do the job cheaper for the very practical reason that contracting with you would enable him to be at home every week on a regular schedule – a rare luxury for an independent trucker. Everyone wins when suppliers are networked into milk runs.

Freight network optimization possibilities almost always expand exponentially when outbound shipments to customers are included in the network of milk run possibilities. Far too often companies treat inbound and outbound freight separately, cutting themselves off from the possible synergies the combined network offers. But when the entire logistics equation is considered, an entirely new level of supply chain integration is possible.

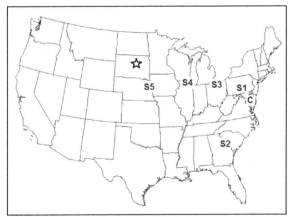

The map to the right shows an actual integrated milk run as practiced by a defense contractor in South Dakota. They made weekly truckload shipments to a customer in Baltimore. The truck then went a short distance to a supplier in Pennsylvania to pick up a week's worth of parts, then down to South Carolina, then to Cleveland, then Michigan, and finally to Omaha before returning to South Dakota.

Along the way, one week of all of their major, high cost components were picked up. They accomplished one week's production out and one week's material in at the lowest possible overall freight cost. Inventory was kept constantly in balance, as inbound material and outbound shipments were integrated into one freight route.

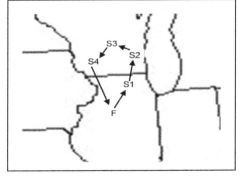

Most milk runs are more local, as indicated by the map and route on the right. In this case, a company in northern Illinois has a daily run which stops at three southern Wisconsin and one northern Illinois supplier, bringing materials needed for the next day's production to the plant.

This points to geography as a very important input to the supply chain. Referring to the map below, showing the company in Arkansas with twelve widely dispersed suppliers, you can see a supplier in southern California, some 1,500 miles from Arkansas. There are no other suppliers along the way, and the closest supplier to the southern California one is in Washington – two days by truck to the north and even further from Arkansas. Unless there are customers along the way that can be combined with inbound shipments there is little that can be done to mitigate the high freight cost versus high inventory dilemma.

This illustrates the need to consider geography in supplier selection. Far too often companies make the mistake of over-simplifying freight - lumping all of their freight costs together and treating it as a one-number percentage addition to their material costs – say 4%. 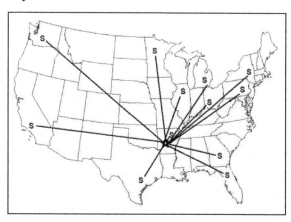 Purchasing ignores the real freight cost, looking solely at purchase price. Someone in the shipping department or a freight manager is then tasked with negotiating freight arrangements to keep the actual freight costs as low as possible, and measures their success by comparing actual results with this preset number.

The weakness in this approach is that it ignores the basic structural problems that ignoring the geographic network can create. The actual freight cost (or its equivalent in the cost of carrying excess inventory) may well add 10% to the cost of the material – an unavoidable condition due to the location of the supplier.

The basic structure of the supply chain and its speed and cost are very much driven by geographic logic. Clustering suppliers along the lines between the operation and major customers can optimize freight costs and minimize inventory. It can greatly improve responsiveness.

It is also important to keep in mind that freight and logistics are 100% non-value adding costs. They may well be necessary costs, but they do not make the product any more valuable to the end customer. The objective is to minimize them (keeping in mind that inventory and its associated costs is also non-value adding and it does not make sense to save $1 in freight if doing so incurs $2 in inventory costs). The question of whether you or your supplier, or you or your customer should be responsible for freight costs and freight management should be based on whose network is more efficient.

There is no efficient way for the Arkansas based manufacturer or distributor to optimize the freight cost from that California supplier. But, perhaps that supplier has multiple customers and suppliers along the route from California to Arkansas. In that case, the supplier should manage the freight since they are better positioned to minimize the cost. It is a mistake to ignore freight expenses by simply adopting a policy of having suppliers pay for freight. Some times that makes sense; most times it does not.

In-source versus Outsource

There is no shortage of firms in the Third Party Logistics business only too willing to take over some or all of the activity before inbound material reaches your facility, and between you and your customers. This can be a critical decision for most companies and should be made very diligently.

The problem with outsourcing logistics is that it makes more sense when the supply chain is viewed as a set of independent silos with no significant interconnection. The reality is that there is no way to carve out a piece of logistics without having it impact the other elements of the supply chain. Third party logistics 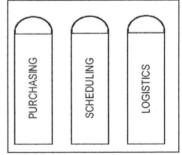 providers are usually experts at freight and warehousing, but know little about your supply strategy or its execution, and even less about how you schedule and manage flow through your operation. In their effort to optimize execution and cost within the logistics silo they can cause a great deal of harm to the rest of the supply chain.

It is for this reason that outsourcing the execution of your logistics efforts almost 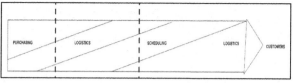 always makes more sense than outsourcing the management of it. You should design your logistics process in the manner that optimizes the entire supply chain and then consider whether outsourcing elements of the execution make sense. Only when you have determined the optimum flow from your operation to your customer's are you ready to sit down with UPS or FedEx, or with a common carrier freight company to discuss the costs and execution of that flow.

The population of the United States is far from being evenly distributed. The populations of Canada and Australia are even less evenly distributed. This means that, for many companies, their customers are clustered somewhere far from their own location.

A west coast company is apt to have many customers in the east – near each other, but far from a California company. Inversely, the eastern company may have quite a few customers in the west, a long way from their location, with very few customers in between.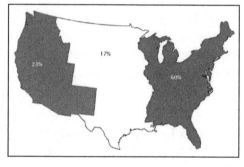

The combination of freight costs and customer lead times may lead to the need for a distribution center where clusters of customers are a long way from the plant. If it is solely a matter of freight costs and lead times are not an issue (for instance, it takes four days to ship from a plant in Los Angeles to customers in the East, but those customers allow one week lead 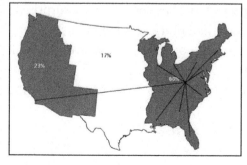 times) a remote warehouse would not make sense. Instead, a freight arrangement that enables truck loads from the west to go to an east coast facility where it is then broken down into smaller shipments for individual customers is more economical.

On the other hand, if the customers in the east require three day lead times, there is no avoiding the need to keep inventory in a location closer to those customers. Whether it makes sense to outsource that warehousing and distribution work to a third party is strictly an economic question. Usually that question comes down to volume and whether the company wants to perform any value adding work at the remote facility. If volumes are relatively low it almost always makes more sense to outsource the warehousing and distribution to a third party firm that will use space in an existing distribution facility, with an existing operational infrastructure. If volumes are high enough to justify the investment and expense of operating a stand-alone warehouse then it may be more economical to operate it without the services of a third party.

If the firm determines it is advantageous to do some value adding work at a remote facility – for instance they might want to ship in bulk and pack the items at the remote facility to minimize freight costs; or they might want to ship components and do both final assembly and packaging remotely – the decision might change. Even if volumes are not sufficient to otherwise justify operating the facility itself, concerns for quality or protecting proprietary technology may over-ride the decision to outsource the work.

Overseas Logistics Concerns

Logistics concerns for materials sourced overseas involve complexity and decisions that can (1.) put particular stress on some elements of supply chain strategy; and (2.) may well change the basis for the in-sourcing versus outsourcing decision.

Typically, the lowest cost freight is via boat, and the highest cost is air freight, with trucking falling in between. With Asian, Australian, South American, African or European suppliers into the United States, trucking is not an option, leaving only the extremes of boat versus air. A surprising number of firms, when considering the inventory investment, costs and lack of flexibility ocean freight creates, opt to use 100% air freight from Asia. Most, however, ship by container via ocean freight.

While we urged senior management to stay on top of the economics and politics of foreign countries where suppliers may be located, supply chain professionals must exert a great deal of effort to learn geography and local transportation networks. In China, for instance, the high volume ports are near Hong Kong and Shanghai, with huge industrial complexes extending inland from each of them. However, these cities and industrial regions are a long way from each other, and the Chinese logistical infrastructure is much better east/west than it is north/south. A supply strategy should be  based in either the Shanghai region and use the Shanghai ports, or in the Hong Kong region and use those ports. Sourcing some parts in both regions makes consolidating shipments very difficult and costly. It is not sufficient to just source from 'China'. Exactly where in China is very important.

The principle is no different than the geographic significance of supply chain network design within the United States. The difference is in the consequences of poor planning. In light of the high cost of ocean freight over thousands of miles, and the substantially longer lead times driving substantial amounts of inventory, ignoring geography is a potentially huge drag on the supply chain. Given the example above, a firm that sources in both the Shanghai and Hong Kong regions and cannot economically consolidate will face the dilemma of either bringing in far more inventory than it needs in order to get sufficient container load rates, or pay very high costs for partial container loads.

Considerable outsourcing of overseas logistics is unavoidable in all but the biggest firms. In order to import materials, a freight forwarder is needed in both the shipping and receiving ports, as well as a customs broker. Typically an importer will use one of the many firms that can provide all of these services in both ports until they reach a volume and comfort level to justify contracting with separate service providers and managing the overall process themselves.

Just about every company that decides to explore an off-shore sourcing strategy finds that it is more expensive and complicated than they expected. While it is much easier for a U.S. based firm to import from NAFTA countries – Mexico and Canada – even this is much more complicated than buying from domestic sources. The supply chain manager should be sure to thoroughly explore all of the costs and flow chart all of the movements, import and export forms and costs, and understand the entire flow in detail before committing to an offshore sourcing process.

CHAPTER 31
Integrated Quality Control

While a detailed discussion of the quality control process is well beyond the scope of this book, it is impossible to design and execute an effective supply chain without thoroughly integrated quality controls. Thus far, the math and logic we have outlined for determining inventory and lot size levels has assumed that all of the products and materials flowing through the supply chain are in good, usable form. To the degree that this is not the case, the supply chain will not meet its fundamental objective of providing products to customers with the smoothest and most economical flow into and through the business without additional inventory being placed throughout the supply chain as a buffer for poor quality. That approach – adding unnecessary inventory to protect the system against unexpected defects is costly and an inefficient use of resources.

While the need for excellent quality is well understood by supply chain professionals who have seen their supply chain execution processes suffer from poor quality, many do not understand that excellent quality is not possible without consistent, short cycle time supply chain execution. There is a mutually supportive relationship between supply chain performance and quality performance.

The Supply Chain – Quality Dynamic

Any good quality system is based on the assumption that defects will occur. Certainly much can and should be done in the product and process design effort to assure that processes are robust enough to withstand a wide range of errors before those errors translate into 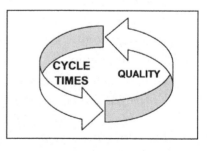 defects, however, the processes are made up of human and mechanical activities. Humans inevitably make mistakes and machines eventually wear out or malfunction. Things will go wrong, so just as important as the design of the quality system to preclude errors is its ability to catch errors and trace them back to the source of the error and then take effective action to learn from the defect and improve the process to minimize the probability of it occurring again. Time is the primary driver of the successful execution of that feedback and corrective action loop.

Consider the example shown below. A process makes ten different items every week. Operation #1 produces in batches of 50, making a batch of two different items each day throughout the week. The output goes to a work-in-process inventory sized to hold a week's worth of production. Finally Operation #2 pulls from the buffer and produces in batches of 10. It makes 10 of all ten items every day.

If Operation #1 creates a defect today (Day 1), that defective product will go into the work in process buffer where it will

	OPERATION #1 Production Schedule - Week 1					Inventory	OPERATION #2 Production Schedule - Week 1				
	MON	TUE	WED	THU	FRI		MON	TUE	WED	THU	FRI
Item A	50					50	10	10	10	10	10
Item B	50					50	10	10	10	10	10
Item C		50				50	10	10	10	10	10
Item D		50				50	10	10	10	10	10
Item E			50			50	10	10	10	10	10
Item F			50			50	10	10	10	10	10
Item G				50		50	10	10	10	10	10
Item H				50		50	10	10	10	10	10
Item J					50	50	10	10	10	10	10
Item K					50	50	10	10	10	10	10

sit for five to six days (assuming we are running on a first in –first out basis), it will then be pulled from WIP and processed in Operation #2 anywhere from 6 to 10 days after the defect was created.

The operator at Operation #2 discovers the defect and a root cause analysis and corrective action exercise is initiated. Because the defect was created 6 to 10 days ago, the likelihood of learning what actually caused the defect is minimal. At that point we may not even know who was working at Operation #1 when the defect was created.

Worse yet, if Operation #1 drifted out of control – if say, the operation is to drill a hole but the fixture wore out and caused the hole to be .01" away from where it was supposed to be – then when the defect is found at Operation #2 we find that everything in process between Operation #1 and Operation #2 is defective.

The basic quality principles this demonstrates are:

- *The more time elapsed between creating a defect and discovering the defect the less likely we are to determine the true cause and take effective corrective action.*
- *The more time elapsed between creating a defect and discovering the defect, the greater the cost of the defect will be.*

The time elapsed in our example between creating and discovering the defect is a function of the batch size at Operation #1 and the size of the work-in-process inventory buffer. In a broader sense the amount of inventory in the supply chain determines the overall cycle time of the supply chain, which is a major driver of the ability of the firm to deploy a successful quality management effort. It is for this reason that, when Motorola first developed and effectively deployed their concept of Six Sigma the driving principle was:

"The best quality producer is the shortest cycle time producer; and the shortest cycle time producer is the best cost producer."

This is based on the idea that excellent quality depends on short cycle times ... and short cycle times depend on excellent quality. The supply chain architect and manager must be keenly aware of his or her critical role in the ability of the company to deploy excellent quality levels. Good quality needs more than just short cycle times, but it is impossible without them.

Formal Quality Programs

In the sections in which supplier selection and management were discussed there was frequent mention of the need for suppliers to have a formal quality management and control process. There are a number of such formal quality management systems; most common is ISO 9001 or one of many variations within the ISO family. It is not so important which particular quality management system a supplier has, as long as the system it uses is thorough and comprehensive, well documented and auditable. A thorough system is one that addresses the responsibilities for quality management for the entire organization, especially management roles and responsibilities (as opposed to a system that is limited to the tasks quality inspectors are expected to complete); a comprehensive system is one that addresses all aspects of quality in the business including product design, suppliers, production operations and information management. The system should be clearly described, and there should be records available demonstrating compliance with the procedures described in that documentation, as well as complete records of quality results. These are minimum requirements, and most serious quality management systems go far beyond these basics.

The intent behind insisting that suppliers have such a formal system is to preclude suppliers whose quality effort is limited to final inspection, or merely reacting to defects after the fact. The primary causes of defects are widely known. They include:

- Poor quality inputs (defective materials from your suppliers' suppliers)
- Poorly designed products (products that cannot be made well regardless of production performance
- Poorly designed processes (processes that rely on incapable machines or are wholly dependent on human perfection
- Poor documentation (missing or inaccurate specifications, poor instructions to production employees, outdated specifications or work instructions, etc…)

A formal quality system recognizes these primary contributors to quality failures and includes proactive measures to address them before they become defects. While you should feel free to recommend one formal quality system approach or another it is not practical to demand that all suppliers conform to one particular quality system or another. The reason is that suppliers have multiple customers and it is often impractical for them to have multiple quality systems in place. For example, a supplier who sells to the automotive industry generally has to comply with the ISO/TS series of quality system requirements; a supplier to the defense industry generally must comply with the MIL-STD series of requirements; there are subsets or variations on ISO systems that address the unique nature of the aerospace, medical, petroleum and natural gas, software and communications industries. The Food and Drug Administration (FDA) also has a comprehensive set of quality standards, as well as 'Best Practices' for the pharmaceutical industry.

For you to dictate that a supplier in compliance with one of those systems must also comply with ISO 9001 to meet your needs is both impractical and unnecessary unless you are in an industry that has such specific regulatory requirements. A supplier in compliance with any of those system requirements has demonstrated sufficient awareness of quality and how to manage it.

ISO 9001

The ISO series is the most widely used, both as a formal system as well as a model for in-house systems. ISO – the International Organization for Standardization – is a worldwide organization (162 member nations) that sets technical standards for a very wide range of items in order to facilitate international exchange and trade, as well as to assure safety. One of their functions has been to set in place a global quality management criteria that enables a company in one country to know that a supplier from the other side of the globe has a quality management system in place that is exactly like the quality management system which that company can see elsewhere.

ISO does not certify companies but registers them. There is a wide range of companies that are authorized to certify companies, and have that certification registered and recognized by ISO. ISO certification and registration requires that a comprehensive documented set of policies and procedures be established and maintained. It often goes well beyond the level of detail a company may think is necessary, and the need to develop and maintain such a thorough document is the primary reason many companies opt to establish an ISO-type quality system but not follow through with the auditing, certification, and annual re-auditing necessary to keep the registration current. This is normally a very expensive proposition and many companies go through the formal certification only if major customers require it.

Whether a company opts to become certified and registered or not, the ISO requirements make an outstanding model for the development of a quality system, and most companies with an effective quality management system have included all of the basic elements of ISO 9001.

Six Sigma and Lean

Recently, many companies have relied on Six Sigma and Lean Manufacturing efforts to manage and control quality. These approaches, however, are completely different animals than formal programs such as ISO. ISO and its variants are truly management systems that address quality very comprehensively – too comprehensively some might say. One frequent criticism of ISO and the like is that it focuses too much on policy and administration of quality than it does on actually finding and fixing defects. Regardless, Six Sigma and Lean are at the opposite end of that spectrum. While a Six Sigma or Lean strategy certainly has profound management implications, as a quality control approach they are primarily tools to analyze and optimize processes in an effort to preclude and eliminate defects and not a comprehensive approach to managing the entire business for excellent quality. If a supplier tells you their formal quality system is an application of Lean or Six Sigma it is necessary to dig deeper to be sure their deployment of Lean and Six Sigma tools comprehensively addresses all four of the primary drivers of poor quality listed above, and that its effectiveness is well documented.

In the end, the deployment of a formal quality system does not assure good quality so much as it assures that good quality is possible. Without a comprehensive approach to quality history has demonstrated that defects are not a matter of 'if' – just a matter of 'when'. It will still be necessary for you to have an inbound quality audit process, regardless of supplier quality in order to elevate your confidence that the suppliers' quality systems are effective.

It should be noted that, while many companies inspect the first few lots from a supplier, or the first few lots of each item, and then when those pass inspection they will generally allow everything from that supplier or all of the particular items to bypass inspection until such time as a defect is found. Then the supplier is put back on an incoming inspection basis until a certain number of lots pass. This practice should only be followed for suppliers that have a validated, capable quality process that includes control of their outbound quality levels. The supply chain must have a very high level of confidence that no defective material is allowed to enter the production or distribution process. The cost and consequences of defects escalates dramatically once defective items have begun to flow through your internal operations.

Incoming inspection should be based on a statistically valid sample plan with a quick, effective follow up with suppliers to disposition any defects, including root cause analysis and corrective action.

An alternative to incoming inspection is a requirement that the suppliers perform the necessary inspections and provide the results of those inspections on a certificate of compliance with each lot. Whether the inspection and validation is performed by the supplier, or by the company, it is imperative that a highly effective quality firewall exists at the receiving dock.

Certain suppliers may be certified and allowed to have their products enter the operation without inspection or proof of supplier inspection. Again, the basis for any such supplier certification must be more than the fact that the supplier has sent some number of shipments without defect. Of course, defect free history is part of any supplier certification criteria, but it must be backed up with firm evidence of a thorough quality management system that is making those defect free shipments happen. Without such a system in place, the defect free lots may well be a matter of good luck or a short term inspection blitz by the supplier to screen problems.

Your Own Quality

Of course the importance of quality for supply chain professionals is not limited to supplier quality. While people in operations are ultimately responsible for the quality of their work, and the company most likely has quality and engineering people responsible for supporting the quality effort, the design of the in-house quality system is of vital importance to the supply chain personnel.

Consider the example of a plant that made refrigeration compressors in North Carolina. One of the areas in the plant made machined components for the compressors and assured that the components do not have even the most minute metal particles on them after the machining operation was critical. In order to be sure they are completely clean, a sample of each day's production gets tested on a mass spectrometer. The actual procedure was for production to accumulate all day and, near the end of the shift, a quality technician would come by and take a sample of the lot to the lab to run the tests. Once the components passed, the lot would be released to go onto the next operation (a sub-assembly process).

While assuring quality was very important – a tiny particle could be enough to make a compressor seize – the design of the inspection process created an extra day in the cycle time. There was rarely, if ever, a defect found. Better alternatives were:

- Have someone in production trained to run the mass spectrometer, then take parts at random throughout the day to be tested and as long as no defects were discovered, allow production to flow directly to sub-assembly

- Reschedule the inspector to come by the machining operations throughout the day and test parts. Again, so long as the parts were good, allow production to flow directly to sub-assembly.
- Essentially to 'certify' the operation since quality was clearly under control (no one could remember the last time a part failed the mass spectrometer test). Allow the parts to flow directly to sub-assembly and have the quality technician test parts at random intervals to be sure quality remained under control.

Any of these approaches would have been preferable to adding a full day to the process cycle time (and a full day's worth of work in process inventory). The designers and managers of the in-house quality system rarely have accountability for inventory levels and do not always have a keen appreciation for the importance of continuous flow. The systems they devise tend to focus on the quality assurance effort alone and often sub-optimize supply chain considerations.

It is the role of the supply chain managers to identify areas in which the supply chain is adversely affected by the quality system and to work with quality leadership to devise more creative approaches that continue to assure quality, but to do so in a manner that does not adversely impact the supply chain.

SECTION IV
Integration, Improvement and Control

This final section includes three chapters in which integrating the supply chain with the new product development effort, operational efforts to continuously improve the business, and management and accounting processes for measurement and control are discussed.

In the new product development area, we address the need to go beyond traditional standard cost focuses for new product criteria and include concerns for how the product will impact supply chain complexity. When the supply chain is properly integrated then introducing products can leverage supplier capabilities, existing inventories, and the logistics network to make the business better. The supply chain can (and should) be a powerful resource to enable new products to be introduced at a lower overall cost, as well as, introducing them faster and more effectively.

In the chapter on continuous improvement we explained how supply chain leadership should be instrumental in driving overall business improvements. In fact, in the early days of our collective understanding of Lean Manufacturing – before the term 'Lean Manufacturing' was even coined as a matter of fact – Lean was understood as Just In Time (JIT) and supply chain leaders were the driving force behind its introduction. The business community has moved away from this supply chain centered approach for a number of reasons, and we describe the central role supply chain managers can play by getting back into a leadership role.

Finally, the standard complement of business measurements – both accounting and non-accounting centered – does not support supply chain improvement adequately. In fact, in many areas those metrics actually encourage degrading the supply chain. In the last chapter we will describe a package of measurements that will help both supply chain leadership and senior managers to track supply chain performance with confidence that improving the supply chain will improve the performance of the entire business.

CHAPTER 32
Product Development and the Supply Chain

Developing new products inevitably has an impact on the supply chain. At the very least a new item must be added to the delivery mix and a determination of whether that product will be made to order or made to stock must be made. More significant is the impact the new product will have on purchasing, logistics, and inventory management ahead of finished goods. In addition to optimizing the impact new products have on the supply chain, early integration of the new product development process with the supplier base can significantly reduce the time from concept to market and increase the probability of the product's initial design success.

Supply Chain / Product Design Principles

There are three basic principles that, when carefully considered in the product design effort, can have a significant impact on the overall cost of the product. The first of these is minimization of new components parts and materials. To the maximum degree possible, existing components should be used, and the number of new item numbers created for the supply chain to manage should be kept to the least possible. Of course, minimizing the total parts count of all types (existing and new) in a new product is an important objective; and the best way to minimize new parts is usually to minimize total parts. Assuming the value of designing products with the fewest parts is well known we will concentrate on the impact of new parts.

Accounting systems typically do not make the cost of adding new parts clear. Let's say, for example, a company currently makes four variations on their Gadget – Products A, B, C and D. They are now creating a fifth version – Product E. Each of these products has a different colored switch:

Product A	Item 1	Blue switch	35¢
Product B	Item 2	Red switch	33¢
Product C	Item 3	Green switch	36¢
Product D	Item 4	Black switch	34¢

In planning the design of Product E, they can either use the switch from Product D – the Black switch that costs 34¢ - or they can specify and entirely new switch – Item 5 that will also cost 34¢. Because the product cost seems to be the same, the marketing and design people may decide to go with a new black switch simply because it is different. It doesn't really impact the product, its performance or the customer's perception, but creating another point of differentiation is often perceived to be a good thing, especially when the cost is the same.

Further, let's assume all of the switches come from the same supplier with a four week lead time, and the order interval is one week (you place an order on that supplier every week). Finally, we will assume sales and marketing has said they expect the new item to sell in volumes and order frequencies comparable to Product C.

Consider this chart showing the inventory analysis for all of these components:

		Item 1	Item 2	Item 3	Item 4	Item 5	Items 4&5 combined	Items 1 - 4	Items 1-5	Items 1-3 + 4&5 combined
Week	1	75	250	100	0	100	100			
Week	2	150	300	125	0	125	125			
Week	3	125	200	75	0	75	75			
Week	4	100	225	75	275	75	350			
Week	5	175	250	125	0	125	125			
Week	6	75	275	75	0	75	75			
Week	7	125	300	75	0	75	75			
Week	8	150	325	175	225	175	400			
Week	9	50	250	75	0	75	75			
Week	10	100	200	75	0	75	75			
Week	11	150	275	75	0	75	75			
Week	12	175	300	125	0	125	125			
Week	13	75	200	75	0	75	75			
Week	14	125	225	150	0	150	150			
Week	15	200	200	75	0	75	75			
Week	16	175	275	75	275	75	350			
Week	17	75	250	75	0	75	75			
Week	18	100	200	75	0	75	75			
Week	19	125	200	200	0	200	200			
Week	20	175	275	75	0	75	75			
Week	21	150	225	75	0	75	75			
Week	22	100	300	75	0	75	75			
Week	23	50	200	75	0	75	75			
Week	24	175	275	150	275	150	425			
Week	25	125	275	75	0	75	75			
Week	26	150	250	75	0	75	75			
Cumulative Lead Time		4	4	4	4	4	4			
Customer Lead Time		0	0	0	0	0	0			
Order Interval		1	1	1	1	1	1			
TOTAL		3,250	6,500	2,500	1,050	2,500	3,550	13,300	15,800	15,800
AVG		125	250	96	40	96	137			
2.2σ		93	87	80	213	80	245			
Inventory		312	423	257	467	257	627	1,459	1,716	1,619

Using the formula from Chapter 17 we have determined that existing items 1-4 behave as indicated in the chart, and we have calculated their target inventory levels accordingly. In the column headed Items 1-4 we can see the total volume over the 26 week period is 13,300 units for the four existing items, and a total inventory for the four items is 1,459 in order to assure our 98%+ availability level.

If we were to simply add another item – Item 5 – behaving exactly the same way Item 3 behaves, our sales volume will increase to 15,800, and the total inventory will go up to 1,716. This equates to a 19% increase in unit volume and about the same – an 18% increase in our inventory of switches.

On the other hand, if we were to use the black switch –Item 4 – on the new product, when we add the planned volume for the increase in volume to the existing volume, keeping the planned order pattern, we find that the sales volume still goes up by 19% to 15,800, but the inventory only increases to 1,619 – an 11% increase.

The reason the increase in volume does not create a corresponding increase in inventory when we use the existing component is the 'flattening effect' combining the total variation for the two items has on the total.

Referring again to the previous chart, you can see that the average demand for Items 4 and 5 is about the same when they are added together: Item 4 averages 40 per week, while Item 5 will average 96 per week. Combined into one item they will average about the sum of the two: 137. The 2.2σ figures are lower when they are combined. Item 4 has a 213 variation figure and Item 5 has a variation figure of 80. Combined they should be 293, but you can see they actually combine to generate a 2.2σ figure of only 245. This is due to the fact that, inevitably, there are weeks in which an increase over the average for one item is offset by a decrease from the average in demand for the other. There is a synergy that usually occurs when items with fairly high variation are combined, as is the case here.

There are certainly many exceptions driven by different possible demand patterns, but as a general rule the total inventory will increase at a lower rate than sales volumes increase when existing components can be used versus the inventory that would result from adding a new component to the supply chain.

The second driving principle is that the addition of new suppliers should be minimized. The reason for this is fairly straightforward, and it is based on the logistics logic discussed in Chapter

27. The map on the previous page shows the supplier network we used as our example in Chapter 27 when the network optimization complexities were discussed. The difference is the addition of a new supplier located in North Carolina.

There is no avoiding the reality that the addition of another supplier will create another necessary stop in the freight route. If the new supplier is located very near other suppliers the additional freight cost from adding a new supplier can be limited to having to make another stop on a milk run, but there will inevitably be additional cost and additional in transit inventory.

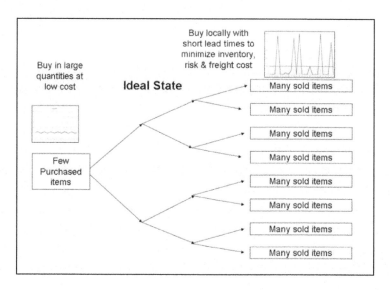

When the supplier is not in a location conducive to a milk run, the increase in freight costs will be more substantial. Just how substantial then becomes a function of the anticipated volumes and the distance from the destination.

Of course, the additional costs of the transactions between you and your suppliers are also very real. An additional supplier means additional contracts, purchase orders and releases. It means additional invoices to be processed, and it means an additional supplier qualification and quality assessment expenses.

Once again these costs do not clearly show up in standard costing analyses. The additional supplier may be able to provide the new black switch at 30¢, rather than the 34¢ the existing supplier quoted. The tendency to ignore the overall cost of a new supplier is aggravated by the practice of treating freight costs as an across-the-board percentage add-on, rather than a discrete cost for each part. The additional freight cost for an existing supplier is virtually nothing. The additional freight cost for a new supplier is probably much higher than the overall freight average.

The third and final principle driving the supply chain considerations in the product development process is that design differentiation should take place as near to the end of the manufacturing process as possible. The most effective supply chain scheme is one that supports a manufacturing scheme that goes from a small number of common, basic platforms, with each platform expanding out into a wide range of customer specific end products. The chart indicating this principle is shown on the previous page, and indicates the process of product differentiation from a relative few purchased items at the start of the process to a broader number of items as the process nears completion.

As a general principle, the few purchased items entering the beginning of the process can be bought further from the plant because they are bought in high volumes. That high volume material is relatively safe inventory because it can go into a wide range of products if the demand for any one end item falls off.

To the right of the process are the items that are bought in low volumes. Freight is more of an issue and the inventory carries a higher risk. Purchase price should be less important for these items, and the best supply chain practices are to buy them closer to the plant and in smaller quantities.

As the small inset charts indicate, because of the synergistic effect described previously, the demand for the few items that go into a wide range of items tends to flatten out, which enables smoother flow with less inventory, while the product specific items used toward the end of the process tend to have more variation in demand. Because the basic items have flatter demand profiles, longer lead times can be tolerated. Inversely, because the lower volume items used at the end of the process have greater variation in demand, it is important to keep lead times as low as possible, hence the importance of purchasing them closer to the plant.

Design Process Considerations

The actual design process itself is one that the supply chain can enhance to a very large degree if the supply chain is well constructed. The key is to have capable suppliers, an understanding of which ones can be critical to the overall product design process, and a willingness to involve them early.

There are two objectives when involving suppliers in the product development process (1.) to take advantage of their own product and (2.) process technology knowledge, and to shorten the design cycle time through concurrent development efforts.

When suppliers are brought in near the beginning of the product development process there is certainly an opportunity to learn about any advances in the materials they have available, or new component capabilities. No matter how capable and informed your engineers are, it stands to reason that the technical people in the suppliers' organizations know more about their specific technology.

More often than the technical assistance the supplier might potentially provide, the real contribution suppliers can make through early involvement is their knowledge of their production processes. A slightly different angle or dimension on a component, or a different grade of steel or aluminum, or a different type of resin may have no bearing on the product being designed but will enable the supplier to make the component at a much lower cost. It is for this reason that virtually all of the suppliers should be brought in and shown the new product at its earliest stages. Too many companies assume the only suppliers to involve are those with critical technical input.

The second vital reason for involving suppliers early is to shorten the product introduction cycle. Stamped, molded, or other parts requiring

When Cincinnati Microwave designed the first consumer radar detector product, they went from concept (commitment to an idea on a white board) to market in 13 weeks. The project began with the firm requirement that the only new supplier would be an Asian source for a few essential photo-electric components. Other major suppliers were brought in to discuss the design idea, and the suppliers' first part lead times. Based on those discussions, the project plan required the design engineers to commit to:

- the precise photo-electric components three weeks into the project
- the overall rough dimensions of the plastic casing immediately in order for the supplier to procure necessary tool steel
- the rough dimensions of the casing within three weeks
- the final dimensions of the casing within five weeks in order to get the molding tool completed
- the outside dimensions of the printed circuit board to be finalized within five weeks
- the final specifications for the printed circuit board to be finalized within nine weeks

A supply chain person was assigned to the effort on a full time basis and that person coordinated design efforts with the lead time requirements for all of the other suppliers. While having to commit to various dimensions and specifications before the design was complete made the design effort more difficult, the result was producing and shipping 110,000 units per week within three months of having a basic product concept.

tooling; parts requiring new materials (new to the supplier, anyway); new printed circuit boards; and a number of other types of parts and materials often have extensive first part lead times. By facilitating supplier participation in the product development process, supply chain leadership can work with the design team to finalize the design of tooled or other long lead time components of the new product and begin work on them early enough to keep supplier work off of the critical path to design completion.

The worst approach to product design is to have one's engineers design the product entirely on their own, then throw it 'over the wall' to the supply chain for competitive bidding in search of the lowest cost. However, world class integration of product design with the supply chain requires management such as that at Cincinnati Microwave and suppliers as capable as Stainless Design.

The traditional, 'purchase price only' approach to product development was the one practiced by a food machine manufacturer in New Zealand. Stainless Design, a local stainless steel fabricator, wanted very much to gain the machine builder's business but they were repeatedly told they were too expensive – the machine builder could have all of the components built in China much cheaper.

The owner of Stainless Design approached the owner of the machine company with a proposition: he would put an engineer in the machine builder's design office at his own expense in return for a chance to quote the next machine they sold. The input the engineer provided resulted in such a radical improvement in quality and reduction in overall cost that Stainless Design became the sole source for the machine builder from that point on. Once the relationship was formalized, Stainless Design was also able to radically reduce the machine builder's lead times to its customers.

The reason Stainless Design was able to make such a contribution was simple. While the machine builder knew food processing technology inside and out, they did not know nearly as much as Stainless Design about all of the different grades of stainless steel available, their cost, their strength in different configurations, or, most important, the manufacturability of various materials in different configurations. At every turn, the Stainless Design engineer was able to offer suggestions for alterations to the part geometry, material specified, or both that would result in better quality at a much lower cost.

CHAPTER 33
Continuous Supply Chain Improvement

In order to manage and continuously improve the supply chain it is essential to understand the fundamental economic principles underlying Lean Manufacturing, and how they differ from the economic concept of traditional supply chain management.

Until the advent of Lean, the financial management of inventory was based on the ideas that:

- Inventory is an asset and therefore does not have a direct impact on the profitability of the business.
- Increasing inventory can be a positive to the business if the 'carrying cost' of inventory does not exceed reductions in labor and purchase prices that can be gained by the increase.
- Sufficient inventory allows each element of the supply chain – suppliers and various production operations – to work independently of each other. They can work at different rates on different products to optimize their own direct costs without regard to the pace of upstream or downstream operations because there is sufficient inventory to buffer them from each other.
- Independently of profits, inventory should be kept to a level that it does not create a cash flow problem for the business.

Inventory carrying costs have been traditionally defined as (1.) the physical warehousing costs directly related to the inventory; (2.) the financial costs of the inventory (such as the 'opportunity costs' or most commonly the lost interest income from having the cash instead of inventory); and (3.) costs related to potential inventory loss or shrinkage.

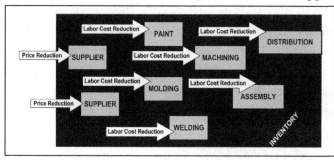

These inventory carrying costs are typically in the 5-15% range. Using the inventory carrying cost as the only negative offset to possible labor efficiency improvements from batch manufacturing or lower purchase prices from bulk purchasing led to the widespread use of those practices, and single digit inventory turns (often low single digits) became common.

Lean is based on an altogether different view of inventory. Actually it is not based on inventory at all – it is based on the idea that cycle time (the amount of time it takes for material to flow from end to end through the entire process) – is the critical indicator of performance. Inventory is simply the result of cycle times. If the factory or distribution center ships 10 of an item per day to customers, and there are 200 of those 'somethings' in inventory, then the cycle time is 20 days. That is to say the next one of those 'somethings' that come into the factory or distribution center will take 20 days, on average, to flow through the entire process before it leaves.

In fact, Lean centers on the Lean Ratio. The Lean Ratio is the amount of time value is being added to material as a percentage of the total time the material is in the process. Typically material is only actually being processed for a matter of a few hours – often only minutes – as a percentage of several days flowing through the plant. Lean Ratios of 1% or less are common.

The concept of Lean is that all of the non-value adding time – the 99% or so – is creating waste … material handling, excess floor space and the associated utility costs, paperwork generated to track and control it all, and on and on. And as was explained in Chapter 28, it is less and less possible to achieve high quality levels. Compounding all of these problems is that customer lead times are being stretched out.

The basic economic principle of Lean is to treat just about everything other than direct materials as a fixed cost, then work to identify and decrease (or eliminate) all costs that are not making the product more valuable in the eyes of customers; and to simultaneously work to steadily increase the rate at which product flows across

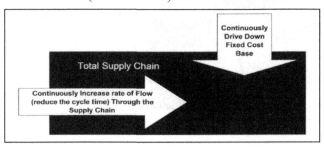

that steadily decreasing cost base.

Improving the supply chain means an improvement in the 'end to end' process – typically this means from the time it leaves your supplier's last value adding operation until it arrives to your customer. This 'end to end' process approach is critical to supply chain improvement because it precludes merely moving inventory from one place to another without improving the total supply chain flow.

Note that, in "*Seeing the Whole: Mapping the Extended Value Stream*" Jim Womack and his co-authors very appropriately urged defining the 'end to end' process as beginning with the raw materials being extracted from the earth through as many suppliers as there may be in the sequential process to getting it to your operation in the form you buy. The point is that the total cost and quality of the materials and goods you buy are a function of everything that happened in its journey to you – not just the actions of the last supplier in the supply chain before you. This is absolutely true and, if it is possible, the supply chain improvement effort should extend further up the supply chain than the last supplier. From a practical standpoint, however, the best most companies can really do is to work with their most recent supplier, and assure that the suppliers they work with are looking further up the supply chain and assuring the highest value possible.

The Figure below indicates the transition many companies go through as their understanding of the concept of 'end to end' processes matures:

	Pre Lean	Early JIT	Tactical Lean	Holistic Lean
SUPPLIER	0	1000	1500	500
PURCH INV	1000	0	500	500
OP 1	0	0	0	0
WIP	500	500	500	100
OP 2	0	0	0	0
FG INV	2000	2000	1000	500
TOTAL INVENTORY				
Company	3,500	2,500	2,000	1,100
Supply Chain	3,500	3,500	3,500	1,600
TOTAL CYCLE TIME*				
Company	35	25	20	11
Supply Chain	35	35	35	16
* assuming average sales of 100 per day				

From a starting indifference towards inventory driving them to carry substantial purchased inventories in order to get low purchase prices, many companies embraced 'Just In Time" as a strategy to do little more than push inventory back on suppliers. Note in the previous example, from the top "Pre-Lean Supply Chain Flow" to the next step – "Early JIT Thinking" - there are still 4,300 units in the total inventory and the time from the last supplier operation to customer shipment was still 43 days. Since the underlying causes of waste in the supply chain were not addressed, the overall cycle time and resultant inventory (and the total supply chain cost) was not really improved.

The next evolution in thinking quite often has been limited to the application of pull systems, or kanbans, to speed up flow through the factory, as well as from the supplier. Note again, in the transition from Early JIT Thinking to "Lean Without End to End Thinking" the result has been limited to pushing the same inventory off of the factory floor back to the purchased inventory or ahead to finished goods inventory, but the overall inventory and cycle time has not improved. This does not really improve the supply chain much (if at all) and it is why many companies claim to have successfully deployed Lean practices while showing little improvement in overall inventory turnover.

It is only in the last stage – "True Lean Thinking" – when firms understand the objective is to improve the overall process – from end to end – rather than isolated segments of it that firms really begin to see true supply chain improvement, and real reductions in overall supply chain cost and quality.

The tools of Lean were developed specifically to facilitate reduction in the cycle time of the end to end supply chain process and, in many regards the essence of this book has been to provide a guide for the application of the fundamental Lean tools and principles to the supply chain.

The next chart defines the basic logic of supply chain improvement, and it applies to a distribution supply chain as well as a manufacturing supply chain. The starting point is to gather the data as it was laid out in the above example of the transition in supply chain management maturity. That is, to create a basic flow chart (value stream map) of the end to end process for any given item flowing into the supply chain, and add to it the normal inventory levels at each step. Based on the average daily shipments of that item (no matter which or how many different end items it may be embedded in when it is shipped to customers).

The next step is to analyze whatever the biggest block of cycle time – or inventory – is and run through the logic above to determine the root cause of the need for the inventory and identify the appropriate tool or technique to eliminate the cause.

Lot Sizing

Large blocks of inventory are always due to either the perceived need for producing things in batches or large lot sizes, or due to problems. The solution to large production batches, as we described in Chapter 19 is the set of set-up and change-over techniques described as SMED – Single Minute Exchange of Dies.

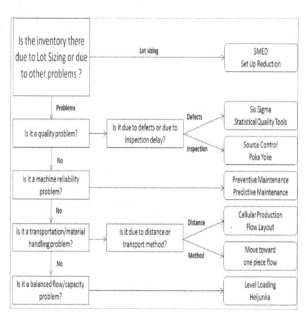

Note that, when the factory aggressively pursues the heijunka concepts described in Chapter 19 these problems will be consistently identified and improved.

The problems that may be causing large blocks of inventory other than batch sizes include transport issues, machine reliability, unbalanced capacity, and quality issues.

Material Handling Methods

Often inventory is the product of the methods used to handle material – overly long conveyor systems, for instance, tend to be stockpilers of inventory. Bins, boxes, pallets and other material handling devices may hold more inventory than is actually necessary to support the flow, and there is a tendency to fill the device, rather than 'right size' the amount being transported.

Distance

A huge driver of wasted supply chain expense is distance. This is the case whether it is a poor factory layout with excessive distances between one operation and the next, or due to the distance between the supplier and the factory or distribution center. In either case, the only way to leverage the transportation cost is often to carry far more material at a time than the amount actually needed. In the case of factory layout, the solution is to rearrange the plant from a functional layout to a value stream flow layout, including the implementation of U-shaped cells. When the problem is the distance from supplier to you, the principles discussed in Chapter 27 apply.

Machine Reliability

This is primarily a manufacturing issue. Excess inventory is carried when there is a high risk of essential machines breaking down; the Lean body of knowledge includes considerable information on the concepts of predictive and preventive maintenance that should be applied.

Due to Unbalanced Capacity

Inventory accumulates when constraints are poorly managed. In Chapter 13 and throughout Section III we discussed scheduling and working with constraints. These ideas are critical when a constraint is the biggest driver of cycle time lost in the overall supply chain. (Note that many experienced manufacturing people maintain they can find the constraint in any factory without the need for data – they simply walk the process and wherever the inventory is piled up the highest is the site of the capacity constraint. This is not always true, but it is more often than not!)

An essential improvement tool is the use of Overall Equipment Effectiveness (OEE) metrics at the constraint. OEE is a method for combining percentages of time equipment is actually usable compared to planned availability; actual production output while the equipment is available compared to output needed to satisfy takt and first pass quality yield.

If the equipment is planned to be available 80 hours per week but due to breakdowns it is only available for production 75 hours, the first element of OEE (availability) would be 94% (75÷80). If during the 75 hours the machine was supposed to produce 4 parts per hour for a total of 300, but it actually only produced 275, the next piece of the OEE equation (output) would be 92% (275÷300). Finally, if of the 275 parts produced it turned out that 20 of them were defective, the first pass yield was only 255 parts, so the last piece of the OEE equation (yield) would be 94% (260÷275).

Based on these results the OEE for the constraint machine would be:

$$94\% \ X \ 92\% \ X \ 93\% \ = \ 80\%$$

This OEE rating would indicate that the constraint is only providing 80% of what it should, and would provide direction as to the areas in which improvement efforts must be directed in order to improve the flow.

Defects and the Inspection Process

When the cycle time waste and inventory is the result of quality issues – either real defects or a poorly designed quality control system as was discussed in Chapter 28 – obviously a concerted application of improved quality methods is necessary. We cannot begin to describe an effective total quality control system in these pages, but the objective must be to gain control of quality at the source, and the starting point should be the operation at the root of the reason for the excessive inventory – whether it is at a supplier location or in your own plant.

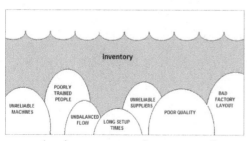

The driving principle is that the application of this approach – find the blocks of dead cycle time, get to the root cause, and eliminate the problem – is the water and rocks theory brought to life. Inventory equates to cycle time – more inventory, longer cycle time means more problems covered up. Those problems are the cause of expenses that drive up overall supply chain costs without adding value customers are willing to pay for, and makes the firm less competitive.

The objective of supply chain leadership is to identify areas of poor supply chain flow and work with the rest of the organization to devise solutions for the good of the company.

CHAPTER 34
Financial & Non-Financial Measures of Supply Chain Performance

On Time Delivery

The most critical measure of how well the supply chain is performing is the rate of On Time Delivery (OTD) to customers. There is no benefit to executing a supply chain strategy that meets economic objectives if it does not, first and foremost, fulfill its primary objective of assuring output that satisfies customers.

What constitutes on time performance should be viewed from three angles: (1.) on time to the shipment date requested by the customer, (2.) on time to the design criteria established for the supply chain process, and (3.) on time to the shipment date promised by the company.

Consider the following example:

My car breaks down on Saturday morning and, being something of a shade tree mechanic, I diagnose it and determine that I need a new water pump. I go to the local auto parts store and they tell me the pump I need is not a stock item and they will order one from the warehouse that will be available for me to pick up in three days. I am disappointed that I have to wait, but say OK, so the guy at the car parts store enters my order into the computer. Upon doing so he finds out that the warehouse is out of them too, so it will be five days before I can get my water pump.

Assuming the water pump is, in fact, available for me in five days the store should calculate their delivery performance as follows:

On Time to Customer Request date – 0%. I wanted it on Saturday and they failed to meet that request.

On Time to Process Specifications – 0%. Presumably their warehouse system was designed to have items that are non-stock in the store available three days after a customer asks for one, and due to the stock out situation in the warehouse they failed to meet this objective.

On Time to Promise Date – 100%. They said I could get the water pump in five days, and I was able to do so.

Of these three measurements, delivering on time to customer requests is far and away the most important. The other two are really

213

subsets of OTD to customer requests, or tools to use that provide helpful information in the quest to achieve 100% on time delivery to customer requests. Too many companies only measure delivery performance to their promise date (if they measure it at all) and in doing so make an enormous mistake. In the case described above, if the company were to only measure their delivery to their promise date, they would pat themselves on the back for a job well done while missing a couple of very important points. For one, they would be blissfully unaware of the fact that they have a dissatisfied customer. I needed the part on Saturday and they didn't have it. While they are satisfied with the design and execution of their supply chain I'll be out looking for another car parts store to visit the next time I need a part precisely because of their inadequate supply chain design and execution.

The other key point they would miss is that something is not working in their supply chain scheme. If the supply chain architecture is intended to assure that non-stock items in the stores are available within three days from the warehouse then something clearly went awry. To be sure, no supply chain system can assure 100% on time availability of everything and anomalies will happen. Perhaps my water pump was one of those anomalies. However, without recording the execution miss on the On Time metric they will never know.

The important point to keep in mind with OTD – and every metric, for that matter – is that it indicates the unvarnished truth. It may well be unreasonable for me to expect the local store to carry every water pump configuration possible. When companies compromise their measurements based on rationalizations of what they deem to be reasonable, however, they deny themselves access to critical information.

Perhaps the company will still opt to classify my water pump as a non-stock item, but if they measure themselves honestly and accurately they will be fully aware of the fact that their supply chain process creates a dissatisfied customer by design. If their OTD metric to customer request is only 95%, and can never be 100% by design, then that may be alright. On the other hand, if their OTD to customer request is only 60% that sends a strong message that their architecture is seriously flawed. Unless the company is truthfully measuring OTD to customer requests – no matter how reasonable or unreasonable those requests may seem– they will never know if the supply chain architecture is aligned with market requirements.

There are a couple of ways to measure on time delivery. Consider the example to the right.

One approach is to measure by order – the company received X number of orders and Y number of orders shipped complete by the due date. OTD would be 'Y complete orders' ÷ 'X total orders due'. Obviously

Line	Item	Quantity Ordered	Quantity Shipped
1	Item A	50	50
2	Item B	50	25
3	Item C	100	75
4	Item D	100	100
5	Item E	25	25
TOTAL		**325**	**275**

this order was not complete and would count against the company if they chose to define OTD as orders shipped complete.

Another approach, and perhaps the most common one, is lines shipped complete. In the chart above, Lines 1, 4 and 5 shipped complete. If this were their only order, the company would measure 3 lines shipped complete out of five lines total for an OTD of 60%.

Finally, some companies choose to measure items. Again referring to the chart, the company shipped 275 total items against an order of 325 total items, so they would give themselves an 85% OTD.

The larger the basis for measurement is defined, the more rigorous the metric. In our example, the company looks best when measuring itself at the item level; less so at the line level, and worst at the order level.

The toughest (and as a result most useful) OTD measurement is at the order level to customer request dates. Many companies do not do too well when measured to this level of OTD measurement, but that should not deter them from doing so. You should always measure yourself against a yardstick that is as tough as or tougher than the one your customers use. It is OK to have an internal OTD metric that says you are 90% on time while your customer's measurement says you are 95% on time. The inverse is not acceptable though – to think you are 95% on time by your own measurement criteria, while your customers think you are only 90% leads to a false sense of success.

We stress once again the importance of honest, no excuses measurements. You may have many valid reasons for not losing the twenty pounds your doctor says will put you at a healthy weight. Those reasons, however, do not justify re-calibrating your scales to say you are already at that healthy weight. You may or may not have the ability or desire to act on information indicating you are less than perfect, but if you don't even have the information then continuous improvement toward perfection is almost impossible.

Financial versus Non-Financial measures

The OTD metric is typically referred to as a non-financial measure of performance. The reason for this is that accounting has not devised a simple, clear method of quantifying the financial impact of delivering on time (or not). Make no mistake, however; it is a profoundly financial measurement. Failure to deliver on time results in lost sales, backorder situations that generate additional shipping and administrative work, and excess inventories.

In fact, all measurements of the business are financial measurements. The differences are merely accounting limitations. Accounting has done a generally poor job of determining the financial implications of supply chain management and, as a result, most of the important metrics are among those classified as 'non-financial'. This accounting inadequacy is the result of inventory itself being classified as an asset, as well as standard costing.

Accounting shortfalls

Inventory as an asset really does not mean much in the long term. An asset is an expense that will hit the bottom line just the same as any other expense – it is merely delayed. The fact that inventory can be held in suspension for an open-ended period of time, however, causes accounting to treat it in a radically different manner that makes it appear to be almost free.

The accounting principles that wreak havoc on effective financial management of the supply chain are the 'matching principle' and 'full absorption'. The idea behind the matching principle is that expenses should be matched with the sales they are directly related to. For instance, if you make something for $10 and sell it for $15, the $10 expense and the $15 sale should be correlated – matched – in the same time period. If you showed the $10 expense this month and the $15 sale next month, an investor or banker might mistakenly think the business is very unprofitable this month, and then might mistakenly think the business is overly profitable next month. By carrying that $10 expense incurred this month on the balance sheet, instead of actually expensing it this month, and then charging it to expenses next month when the sale occurs, the expense and revenue are properly matched and that investor or banker will get a clearer picture of the company's level of profitability.

The idea of full absorption is that all expenses related to making that item are excluded from this month's expenses and carried in inventory until the sale is made – not just the straightforward, direct material and labor expenses. This means that many overhead expenses, most of them fixed and most of them only theoretically related to making the product have to be assigned to each product, and then excluded from current expenses, only to be charged later when the products are sold.

Examples of such expenses are supervision, quality control and material handling costs. They are expenses required to produce something, but they don't really change if the factory produces any one particular set of items or another. They are also somewhat fixed over any reasonable period of time, and they do not change as factory volumes go up or down within a fairly broad range of volumes. As a result, any method of assigning a portion of these expenses to each item the factory may produce is, at best, a rough estimate.

As a result of this combination of deferring expenses, and assigning rough approximations to each item as part of the cost to be deferred, using accounting data to manage the supply chain presents some problems.

First is the matter of over and under absorption. As the factory increases inventory, it is taking more of the overhead expenses into inventory than it is expensing with sales. For instance, if each item has $5 of overhead assigned to it, and the factory makes 1,200 items, then $6,000 of this month's overhead goes to inventory (1,200 units X $5 per unit). If sales were only 1,000 units, then expenses were only charged $5,000 for the overhead (1,000 units X $5 per unit). The difference - $1,000 – of this month's actual overhead expense is not deducted from profits, but transferred to inventory to be held there until the items are sold.

If inventory is steadily increased over a long period of time, quite a bit of overhead can be moved into inventory, and while the inventory is increasing, the company can look more profitable than it really is.

The inverse also occurs when inventory is being reduced. Now the company does the opposite – sells 6,000 but only makes 5,000. This creates a situation in which the company must show a $6,000 expense (the overhead assigned to the items sold from inventory), while actual expenses of only $5,000 were incurred and transferred out of expenses. The company now looks less profitable than it really is.

Direct Material	$	5.00
Direct Labor	$	1.30
Variable Overhead		
Unapplied direct labor	$	0.34
Shop Supplies	$	0.51
Machine Maintenance	$	0.30
Quality Control	$	0.26
Material Handling	$	0.21
Utilities	$	0.47
Training	$	0.13
Total Fixed Overhead	$	3.76
TOTAL COST	$	12.29

A supply chain system that continually drives inventory down can make the company appear to be less profitable. Of course, that appearance of lower profitability is not real. The company is merely forced to account for overhead expenses it incurred in the past but was able to defer by putting into inventory. Depending on how great the inventory build-up was in the past, and how much overhead expense was assigned to that inventory, an inventory reduction strategy can have the appearance of a very significant negative impact on profits.

This terribly misleading aspect of accounting drives considerable resistance to best supply chain practices. Reducing inventory enables the company to tie up less cash, reduce the amount of overhead expense required to handle and maintain the inventory, and enables quality improvements – all things that will enable the company to be more profitable. Yet accounting reflects inventory reduction as a negative to short term profits.

It is essential that both senior management and supply chain management be acutely aware of this accounting logic and take it into consideration – expect it and realize it is not actually bad for the business even if it appears so on paper in the short term. It is particularly important that it be considered when creating individual performance measurements that are based on book (or paper) profits. Failure to do so will inevitably cause resistance to the execution of strategies aimed at improving the rate of supply chain flow.

The other problem accounting creates is the result of the logical weakness of standard costs. By allocating generally fixed supply chain costs to individual products, a misleading combination of fixed and variable costs is created as the graphic above indicates.

The material and labor costs are variable, incremental costs. (Many Lean companies and others with a no-layoff policy would argue about the variability of labor costs. They actually deal with the awkward cost behavior of labor being variable with volume increases but fixed with volume decreases). The overhead costs are not incremental, however. Selling more or less of the item will not change the actual spending. This can create difficulties in measuring and managing the supply chain when companies rely on such standard costs to make decisions.

Direct incremental costs lend themselves to incremental decision making, such as make versus buy. Fixed supply chain expenses, however, do not. Those are expenses that are driven by strategy and the choices of supply chain architecture and execution which have been discussed throughout this book.

Whether the company changes the price, outsources production, or makes more or less of the item in the standard cost breakdown graphic, the monthly costs for items such as quality control and material handling will not change. They also appear to be insignificant when viewed as the graphic shows – at the item level. When the company makes business decisions at this item level based on standard costs there is little control over or opportunity for significantly improving supply chain costs.

For instance, if the company sources 30% of its material from China, a fixed supply chain expense structure is put in place. It may include people to plan and manage the sourcing and logistics, and a substantial amount of floor space, racking, material handling equipment and people to manage the inventory necessary to protect long lead times. That cost is spread over everything as the graphic indicates.

If the company makes decisions at this level, a decision to source some of the material locally, rather than in China, will yield little benefit. The material cost will in all probability increase, and there will be no real savings in supply chain costs. The same is true in the case of a decision to replace a single supplier with marginal quality with a supplier with excellent quality. Any increase in the direct, marginal price of the purchased item will not be offset by a savings in quality control costs.

Those costs – supply chain management and control, material handling, quality control, etc… - are driven by the entirety of the supply chain scheme, and can only be substantially reduced by changing that entire scheme. Replace the entire Chinese supply base with domestic suppliers and significant savings can be derived from the resultant inventory decrease. Replace only one supplier and save little or nothing.

Replace all suppliers who have uncertain quality with suppliers who can assure quality and save quite a bit. Replace one and save only a little or nothing.

Take one item from a planner/scheduler driven ERP system and put it into a shop floor controlled kanban and save little. Replace all of the items with such a shop floor execution approach and save quite a bit.

These savings opportunities are rarely seen by companies that are primarily driven in their financial decision making by standard costs with allocated overheads. The potential savings from reduced material handling savings – apparently a maximum of the 21¢ allocated to the item is insignificant compared to the $5 of material or even the $1.30 in direct labor. Saving the 21¢ won't really happen by doing anything with this item alone; and even if it could be eliminated entirely it would be of small benefit compared to the material and labor expenses. It is because of this approach to financial management that many companies focus on outsourcing direct labor and offshoring purchased materials, while ignoring the significant economic benefits possible through an improved supply chain strategy.

As a result of all of these accounting weaknesses the supply chain financial management must be based on actual spending levels compared to budgets and trends (trending is almost always a more accurate indicator of financial control than comparing actual expenses to annual budgets). While managing total supply chain expenses – not washed through inventory and not allocated to products, but actual spending – can assist in controlling and identifying small opportunities for continuous improvement, the big improvements can only come from linking costs to strategy – knowing what the total cost is that exists to support offshore sourcing, for instance – and then evaluating opportunities to eliminate major blocks of such expenses through an alternate sourcing strategy.

Inventory turns – a limited metric

The most common measure of supply chain execution is inventory turnover – typically calculated by dividing an annualized statement of the cost of goods sold (or produced) by the average inventory. This is typically another purely financial metric that can be misleading, at best it is a directionally valid indicator of supply chain management.

The primary weakness of typical inventory turnover ratios is that they are based on financially weighted numbers. It is a useful indicator of cash flow and usage, but a poor indicator of physical flow of inventory, which makes it a limited indicator of inventory management.

Consider the two scenarios in the graphic. In the first one, the inventories encompass 18,000 items, require 12,600 cubic feet of warehouse space, and have a value of $51,000. Based on normal inventory turnover calculation math, this inventory turns at a rate of 5.2 times per year.

Scenario #1

ITEM	COST	CUBIC FEET	INVENTORY UNITS	$$$	ANNUAL SALES UNITS	@CGS	TOTAL CF IN INVENTORY	DAYS ON HAND
A	$ 9.00	0.1	1,000	$ 9,000	6,000	$ 54,000.00	100	43.3
B	$ 3.00	1.0	8,000	$24,000	40,000	$120,000.00	8,000	52.0
C	$ 2.00	0.5	9,000	$18,000	45,000	$ 90,000.00	4,500	52.0
TOTAL		AVG:	6,000	$51,000	91,000	$264,000.00	12,600	86.7

Inventory Turns = $264,000 ÷ $51,000 = 5.2

Scenario #2

ITEM	COST	CUBIC FEET	INVENTORY UNITS	$$$	ANNUAL SALES UNITS	@CGS	TOTAL CF IN INVENTORY	DAYS ON HAND
A	$ 9.00	0.1	2,000	$18,000	6,000	$ 54,000.00	200	86.7
B	$ 3.00	1.0	6,000	$18,000	40,000	$120,000.00	6,000	39.0
C	$ 2.00	0.5	8,000	$16,000	45,000	$ 90,000.00	4,000	46.2
TOTAL		AVG:	6,000	$52,000	91,000	$264,000.00	10,200	86.7

Inventory Turns = $264,000 ÷ $52,000 = 5.1

In the second scenario, the quantity of Item A increased while the quantities of Items B and C decreased. Note that the total items in inventory went down by 11% to 16,000 units, and the warehouse space needed decreased by 19% to 10,200 cubic feet. Even though these primary drivers of materials management and handling expense improved, inventory turnover actually degraded in the second scenario from 5.2 annual turns to 5.1.

The problem, of course, is that this places a high priority on managing expensive items and less on lower cost items, even though the supply chain expense for purchasing cardboard boxes is exactly the same as the cost of buying microprocessors, and the logistics and handling costs of the boxes is likely to be much greater than the same number of microprocessors. Of course, the inverse of scenario #2 is quite likely, as well.

Scenario #3		CUBIC	INVENTORY		ANNUAL SALES		TOTAL CF	DAYS ON
ITEM	COST	FEET	UNITS	$$$	UNITS	@CGS	IN INVENTORY	HAND
A	$ 9.00	0.1	500	$ 4,500	6,000	$ 54,000.00	50	21.7
B	$ 3.00	1.0	9,000	$27,000	40,000	$120,000.00	9,000	58.5
C	$ 2.00	0.5	9,500	$19,000	45,000	$ 90,000.00	4,750	54.9
TOTAL		AVG: 6,000		$50,500	91,000	$264,000.00	13,800	86.7

Inventory Turns = $264,000 ÷ $50,500 = 5.2

In Scenario #3 you can see an increase in the cost drivers of inventory – units and space – with the same financial inventory turns number. The point is that improvement in financial inventory turns results does not necessarily translate into a more effective inventory investment. More importantly, it does not indicate that lower inventory management and handling costs should be expected.

The graphic below includes a column for Days On Hand, which is a much better indicator of overall inventory management. The big difference is that it gives equal weight to all items and has no cost bias. Note the direct correlation between Days On hand rating and the physical factors. The lowest Days On Hand rating is for Scenario #2, which is not only the best case in terms of financial inventory turns, but is the best case in terms of total items and space, as well. Scenario #3 – the one that seems to be neutral in terms of financial turns – is the

Scenario #1		CUBIC	INVENTORY		ANNUAL SALES		TOTAL CF	DAYS ON
ITEM	COST	FEET	UNITS	$$$	UNITS	@CGS	IN INVENTORY	HAND
A	$ 9.00	0.1	1,000	$ 9,000	6,000	$ 54,000.00	100	43.3
B	$ 3.00	1.0	8,000	$24,000	40,000	$120,000.00	8,000	52.0
C	$ 2.00	0.5	9,000	$18,000	45,000	$ 90,000.00	4,500	52.0
TOTAL		AVG: 6,000		$51,000	91,000	$264,000.00	12,600	86.7

Inventory Turns = $264,000 ÷ $51,000 = 5.2

Scenario #2		CUBIC	INVENTORY		ANNUAL SALES		TOTAL CF	DAYS ON
ITEM	COST	FEET	UNITS	$$$	UNITS	@CGS	IN INVENTORY	HAND
A	$ 9.00	0.1	2,000	$18,000	6,000	$ 54,000.00	200	86.7
B	$ 3.00	1.0	6,000	$18,000	40,000	$120,000.00	6,000	39.0
C	$ 2.00	0.5	8,000	$16,000	45,000	$ 90,000.00	4,000	46.2
TOTAL		AVG: 6,000		$52,000	91,000	$264,000.00	10,200	86.7

Inventory Turns = $264,000 ÷ $52,000 = 5.1

Scenario #3		CUBIC	INVENTORY		ANNUAL SALES		TOTAL CF	DAYS ON
ITEM	COST	FEET	UNITS	$$$	UNITS	@CGS	IN INVENTORY	HAND
A	$ 9.00	0.1	500	$ 4,500	6,000	$ 54,000.00	50	21.7
B	$ 3.00	1.0	9,000	$27,000	40,000	$120,000.00	9,000	58.5
C	$ 2.00	0.5	9,500	$19,000	45,000	$ 90,000.00	4,750	54.9
TOTAL		AVG: 6,000		$50,500	91,000	$264,000.00	13,800	86.7

Inventory Turns = $264,000 ÷ $50,500 = 5.2

worst scenario in terms of broader inventory management.

The calculation used in the charts was (Average Inventory for the three items) ÷ (Total Units ÷ 260 work days). If your number of work days is other than five days per week then the figure you use should be adjusted accordingly. Note also that many companies opt to exclude 'C' items – fasteners and similar very low cost, bulk purchased items from their calculation.

Value Stream Mapping Shortcuts

The best tool for measuring and controlling the supply chain is a value stream map – essentially a flow chart that tracks the flow of an item (or a collection of similar items) from the beginning of the supply chain to the end; collecting data along the way regarding cost, quality, time, and resources consumed. The measurement of the supply chain is the sum of all of this data. Improvement in supply chain performance is a reduction in cost, time and resources consumed, as well as improvements in quality.

Because value stream mapping is both time consuming and virtually impossible for companies with hundreds and thousands of items flowing through their supply chains, a couple of short cut indices have been developed to streamline the process. MBILS (pronounced Em-Bills) and the MATI Scorecard (pronounced 'Matty') are simple methods to efficiently collect all of the relevant data and measure performance and the results of improvement efforts. Full blown value stream mapping is reserved for those items that have MBILS and MATI results indicating significant room for improvement.

MBILS

MBILS is a box score method for measuring the flow of items into the plant or warehouse. It stands for:

M – Number of MRP or material system transactions
B – Batch sizes in terms of average day's supply
I – Average day's supply of Inventory in excess of the calculated target inventory
L – Supplier's lead time in days
S – Average days of Inventory required due to variation in demand (The gap between 2.2σ and 0 in the target inventory calculation)

Because most of this data can be easily obtained, calculating an MBILS score for each purchased item is usually not difficult. Improvement in the flow of an item will result in a reduction in that item's MBILS score. The value of the MBILS approach, in addition to simplicity, is its comprehensive nature. It assures that improvement in one aspect of the supply chain is not coming at the expense of another. For instance, lead times are not being reduced by negotiating arrangements with suppliers to bring in bigger batch sizes.

Group: Chair leg blanks						
Item	Description	M	B	I	L	S	Total
A	3.00" Diameter chair legs	4	3	4	6	1	18
B	2.50" diameter chair legs	4	4	1	6	5	20
C	2.25" diameter chair legs	4	6	1	6	7	24
D	2.00" diameter chair legs	4	1	1	9	3	18
TOTAL		16	14	7	27	16	80

The previous graphic shows what a typical MBILS analysis might look like. These are four different diameter blank wooden pieces a company brings in for further processing to make into chair legs.

The analysis for each item might include:

When looking into why Item A requires inventory in excess of the target (an MBILS score of 4 in the 'I' column), the analysis might uncover an ongoing quality problem requiring the safety stock. Supply chain improvement will result from resolving the quality problem without degrading any of the other factors.

Item D comes from a different supplier than the other three items, requiring a much longer lead time. Sourcing it with the same supplier as the other items can result in a shorter lead time, and as a result, a shorter lead time and less inventory.

Note that a total MBILS score is calculated for all of the items in a similar class or commodity. The MBILS scores for Items B and C indicate considerable inventory due to variation in demand. Eliminating Item C and having all of the chairs produced from only three chair leg blanks may allow the demand for Items B and C to be combined. Collectively the demand pattern will be smoother and all of the inventory and transactions for Item C can be eliminated, as well as improving the MBILS score for

Item B as a result of smoother demand and the need for less inventory relative to demand.

All of these items require weekly MRP analysis time for a buyer – a total item class requirement for 16 five or ten minute actions every month. Putting these items into a kanban that enables a shop floor person to simply execute weekly releases will save as much as two and a half hours of buyer workload every month, freeing time for the buyer to do less routine execution work and more time to work on improvement opportunities.

MBILS scores can be summarized a number of ways to measure various aspects of the supply chain. The rate of improvement in total MBILS scores for all items from a supplier is a good indicator of that supplier's participation in supply chain improvement. The rate of improvement in total MBILS scores for all items assigned to a particular buyer is a good indicator of the buyer's management of the supply chain.

The MATI Scorecard

MATI is a companion to MBILS, and in fact, there is some degree of overlap between the two. The purpose of MATI is to measure and facilitate improvement of the interface between the arrival of incoming materials and its introduction to the production process. In the case of distribution centers, it is an effective tool for managing the entire process.

MATI is an acronym for:

Moves – Number of times an item is physically moved
Activities – The number of activities that take place for an item (i.e. counting, inspecting)
Transactions – The number of system transactions that take place
Inventory – Average days of inventory on hand

All of the items in the MATI score are non-value adding waste. The ideal state is for incoming material to be transacted once as having been received, then moved directly to its point of use without the need for further management attention. A poorly designed supply chain process is one that requires multiple material handling, transacting and control activities. MATI is simply a way of measuring the degree to which the system is waste free. As with MBILS, the value is in assuring that an improvement in one area is not offset by degradation in another area. Also similar to MBILS, summaries of MATI scores by the various people and production areas responsible for the flow in that area can serve as an effective measure of their rate of improvement.

Alternate financial approaches

The work embodied in the area of Lean Accounting provides a much more effective financial measurement and control of the supply chain than traditional, standard cost and absorption based accounting. While a comprehensive discussion of Lean Accounting is beyond the scope of this book, the driving principles of Lean Accounting include:

A value stream structure – costs are collected by value streams from beginning to end, cutting across traditional functional silos and cost center lines. This enables management to view all of the costs related to the entire flow, rather than a collection of allocated costs.

An assumption that all costs are fixed and treatment of supply chain costs as period expenses to be tracked and evaluated as they are spent, rather than as they are 'washed' through inventory and matched with sales.

Further, Lean Accounting principles include value based pricing and holistic assessments of make versus buy and capital investment decisions which eliminates the need for standard costing all together.

For an in-depth understanding of Lean Accounting and the financial measurement and control of the supply chain it offers, *Practical Lean Accounting*, *Real Numbers* and *Simple Excellence* are valuable resources.

As weak as traditional accounting is in supporting domestic supply chain management, it is even worse when tracking offshore supply chains. Harry Moser has created an organization called The Reshoring Initiative and has developed what he calls the Total Cost of Ownership estimator. It is intended to be an adjunct to traditional accounting, rather than an alternative, and it serves as a comprehensive guide to all of the financial implications of global supply chains, including the various risks and 'soft costs' that global supply chains drive. (It can be found at www.reshorenow.org.)

Supplier Performance

Extensive and detailed supplier performance metrics are generally used as poor substitutes for a communications-rich relationship with suppliers, and as a result not a good practice. The other problem with them is they tend to require scarce time and effort to generate, and often become the subject of quite a bit of discussion concerning form instead of substance.

The fundamental performance concerns are price, delivery and quality. Most well managed companies do not view these as grades or degrees of excellence so much as pass/fail issues. Suppliers are expected to deliver on time with perfect quality every time. Either they did so or not. Based on this view of the company's expectations of its suppliers, feedback need not consist of any more than a yes/no, good/bad feedback mechanism. In fact, many companies now provide supplier feedback monthly that consists of no more than either a 'smiley face' or a 'frowning face'. In the event of 'frowning face' feedback, it is assumed the supplier is already well aware of any defects or missed delivery dates. Price is assumed to be a well-known matter of ongoing discussion between the company and its suppliers, and no formal feedback is needed.

[i] "Management: Tasks, Responsibilities, Practices" by Peter F. Drucker; Harper Collins Publishers, Inc.; New York, New York; 1973

[ii] *The Goal* by Eliyaho M. Goldratt and Jeff Cox; North River Press: Third Revised Edition; July 2004

[iii] *Theory of Constraints* by Eliyahu M. Goldratt; North River Press; First Edition; December 1999

[iv] "Six Sigma" is a registered trademark and a registered service mark of the Motorola Corporation. This book is not intended to represent a comprehensive description or discussion of Six Sigma; rather, it is limited to the application of a narrow aspect of Six Sigma principles to inventory planning. For a comprehensive understanding of Six Sigma a good starting point is Wikipedia; http://en.wikipedia.org/wiki/Six_Sigma

[v] Harris, F.W. "*How Many Parts To Make At Once*", The Magazine of Management, 10, (1913)

Made in United States
Orlando, FL
11 July 2022

19639069R00127